Contents

Explore visual thinking, geometry, symmetry, logic, computation, factoring, and much more! Find easier worksheets up front, more adventurous worksheets further back.

Puzzles, Challenges, and Activities by Concept

Helping Young People Get Smarter Every Day

Getting Smarter Every Day is a selection of activities, puzzles, ideas, information, and graphics to excite, enrich, challenge, instruct, amaze, and entertain students. This book aims to broaden student perspectives on what mathematics really is and its application in the real world.

Numeracy and *Getting Smarter Every Day*

Wouldn't it be nice if students could "play" with numbers the way they do with balls or musical instruments? Wouldn't it be nice if students had a good feeling for what mathematics really is? Wouldn't it be nice to provide students with mathematics instruction that contributes to *numeracy,* the ability to understand and apply mathematics in everyday life?

Students often see mathematics only as arithmetic, because that is all they have been shown. They see mathematics as a series of algorithms to memorize, then apply to numbers, with a single answer as a result. Mathematics may also seem a solitary subject, without teamwork and sharing. Relatively few students explore the mathematical subjects they encounter, seeing no room for creativity.

Four major instructional approaches break through those barriers to promote numeracy, and *Getting Smarter Every Day* materials encourage and support such approaches.

Discussion and interaction. *Getting Smarter Every Day* presents puzzles that students and teachers will want to talk about. Students learn from each other. An interesting problem may have many parts; so, students with different learning styles may all experience success contributing to a group solution. When mathematics materials offer students opportunities for brainstorming, for enlightened discussion, they can discover beauty and excitement in a subject they will want to explore even further.

Active exploration. Active participation and discovery help students see the concrete aspects of mathematics, setting the stage for later generalization and abstraction. *Getting Smarter Every Day* prompts students to look for mathematical patterns in both numbers and images. When students make such discoveries themselves, they remember the relevant concepts better. Students are more likely to want to explore mathematics when they feel they have an individual role in those discoveries. Mathematics has room for creativity, for multiple methods and approaches.

Visualization and estimation. Everyday applications of mathematics frequently involve visualization and estimation. Students who are visual learners but not strong in math gain greater understanding (and enthusiasm) for mathematics through the many visual-thinking puzzles and activities in *Getting Smarter Every Day* (identified in the activity-concept grid on pages iv and v). Such selections also help students who are not skilled visual learners improve visualization skills. Though *Getting Smarter Every Day* does not specifically focus on estimation, its content involves estimating in many mathematical settings, such as probability, patterns, measurement, and visual perception. Group discussion of specific worksheets can provide many opportunities for exploring the process and value of estimation.

Interrelating concepts. Working on nonroutine, multi-step problems triggers students to use and become comfortable with a holistic approach to finding mathematical solutions. Such an approach requires teachers frequently to tie topics together. Just as a jigsaw puzzle becomes easier as more pieces fit together, so the solution of problems becomes easier as students connect mathematical ideas. Many materials in *Getting Smarter Every Day* involve multiple mathematical issues. The interplay of these issues is shown in the activity-concept grid on pages iv and v.

Overview of *Getting Smarter Every Day*

This is Book C in a series of six books (A through F) in the *Getting Smarter Every Day* series. This book is for students of varying skill levels in grades 4 through 6. Mathematical prerequisites for most activities are basic. (For activities suitable for students not working up to grade level or ability, also see Book B. For activities suitable for students working above sixth-grade level, also see Books D and E.)

Getting Smarter Every Day Book C contains 86 worksheets. They are not intended for use page-by-page in numerical sequence. Rather, "pick and choose," selecting activities for a specific purpose. In general, the difficulty of activities increases from the front of the book to the back. The topics and concepts included often do not appear in regular classroom texts and, admittedly, are favorites of the author. The broad concepts included are:

- computation
- geometric relationships
- logic
- numeration

- part-whole relationships
- pre-algebra
- problem solving
- visual thinking

On pages iv and v, a grid identifies the specific worksheets in *Getting Smarter Every Day* that address each of these concepts. Teachers can use this grid in several ways. For instance, if students enjoy a specific topic or puzzle, the teacher can use the grid to locate similar activities for immediate follow-up that lets the class practice newly-discovered problem-solving techniques.

For even more activities on a topic, *Getting Smarter Every Day* also includes More Smart Books (pages 102 and 103), a list of specific books with related worksheets. This list is keyed to the specific worksheets in this book. Also look at Smart Math Web Sites, on page 104.

Worksheet completion time for the average student varies but generally ranges from 15 to 45 minutes. Perceived difficulty will vary considerably, as ability also ranges considerably in most mathematics classes in this grade range. For a more specific estimate of time requirement, and to assess appropriateness of a worksheet for a specific class, try an activity before assigning it.

Ways to Use This Book

This book is a resource whose pages teachers may use as blackline masters to reproduce worksheets for their own classroom or for specific students. Teachers may also use these pages to create overhead transparencies.

Warm-ups. *Getting Smarter Every Day* worksheet pages serve nicely as warm-up handouts or overhead transparencies. The teacher may give the students 5 to 10 minutes to work on an activity (while handling attendance and homework collection), then have a brief class discussion on questions, ambiguities, and strategies. If needed, the class may complete the worksheet during class time or as regular or optional homework.

Enrichment. In a typical class, student ability and interest spread is amazing. The teacher then faces quite a task to challenge each student. *Getting Smarter Every Day* worksheets serve well as "selected activities" for specific students.

Introduction to a new topic. If students have become accustomed to the style and pace of their mathematics textbook, they may expect the next chapter to feel just like the one preceding it, holding little excitement. As a surprise, teachers can grab student attention by using a relevant problem, puzzle, or activity from *Getting Smarter Every Day*. The challenge of a puzzle often has more motivational appeal than, "Now, turn to page . . ."

Extension or review of a concept. Teachers may use *Getting Smarter Every Day* worksheets to give students extra practice or review of a textbook topic. The worksheets may also provide an application of or connection with a recently-studied topic. A great way to extend a topic is to have students make a problem or a puzzle of their own. Several puzzle formats in this book lend themselves to that kind of extension. Often, students really understand a concept for the first time when they create their own problem.

Bulletin boards. Several pages in *Getting Smarter Every Day* present a graphic image without an activity assignment. Photocopies (perhaps at an enlarged scale) of these images make intriguing bulletin board materials. You may also display copies of such images that students have colored, outlined, or otherwise modified to display a variety of patterns within such images.

Assessing Student Results in *Getting Smarter Every Day*

Though *Getting Smarter Every Day* emphasizes thinking and process, teachers (and students) often want to know the "right" answer to puzzles and challenges. Experience with these materials will show that sometimes, even in mathematics, there is more than one "right" answer.

Answers. Solutions are provided in Smart Answers, starting on page 97. For many of the problems in *Getting Smarter Every Day,* answers are not unique. Praise students who get different answers, if their answers are correct. Use such experiences to help students see that, in the real world, a problem often has more than one correct answer. To extend a good problem, ask, "Is the answer unique?"

To grade or not to grade. Students, particularly students who have a low opinion of mathematics and of their own mathematics ability, often find refreshing math activities that are different, fun, and not graded. Students with an interest in art, for example, who begin to see math applications in art may have an attitudinal change toward mathematics. Students who are not graded on *every* thing they do may welcome the freedom from fear of failure.

Using Special Features in *Getting Smarter Every Day*

Getting Smarter Every Day includes several types of material that present opportunities for exploring mathematics visually without specific assignments.

Grids and dot paper. Many worksheets in *Getting Smarter Every Day* emphasize drawing, sketching, designing, or problem solving. Fun Grids to Copy and Use, starting on page 88, provides several grid and dot masters. Students can use copies of these grids to work on such activities, especially to try extensions on their own. If you do not provide such grids with specific worksheets, let students know that they may request such grids if they want to use them.

Graphic images. Graphic images in *Getting Smarter Every Day* with no specific task assignment are designed to foster student appreciation of the beauty of mathematics. As previously suggested, you may use these as bulletin board material. You may also use such a graphic as a "prop" to ask students to bring in images from magazines, posters, or newspapers. From these contributions, you may create a bulletin board on architecture, sculpture, art, nature, and their connections to mathematics. Over the years, you may accumulate impressive files of pictures that reveal this beauty to your students.

Use of design technology. All the geometric designs in this book were created by the author on the computer using Adobe Illustrator® software. Most computers have some drawing programs. You may use the graphics in *Getting Smarter Every Day* as models for students to create related images with computer drawing programs or by hand.

TIC-TAC-NUMBER

Use the clues to fill in the nine squares in each problem with digits 1–9 (one digit per square).

1.

a. 5 is in the center.
b. No number is in the same row as a number one more or one less than it.
c. 2 and 4 are in the bottom row.
d. 1 and 6 are in the top row.
e. 8 is one square above 5.
f. 9 is in the center column.
g. 3, 4 and 6 are in the right column.
h. 7 is two squares left of 3.

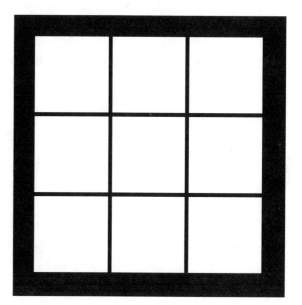

2.

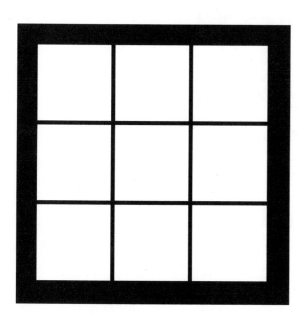

a. All corner numbers are odd.
b. All middle row numbers are even.
c. 5 is one square right of 6.
d. 3 is one square right of 0.
e. 2 is one square left of 8.
f. 1 is in the upper left corner.
g. 7 is one below and one to the left of 8.
h. 4 is one square above 5.

Do you see black arrows or white arrows?

SUM RINGS

Write the sum of the six numbers in the center of each ring.

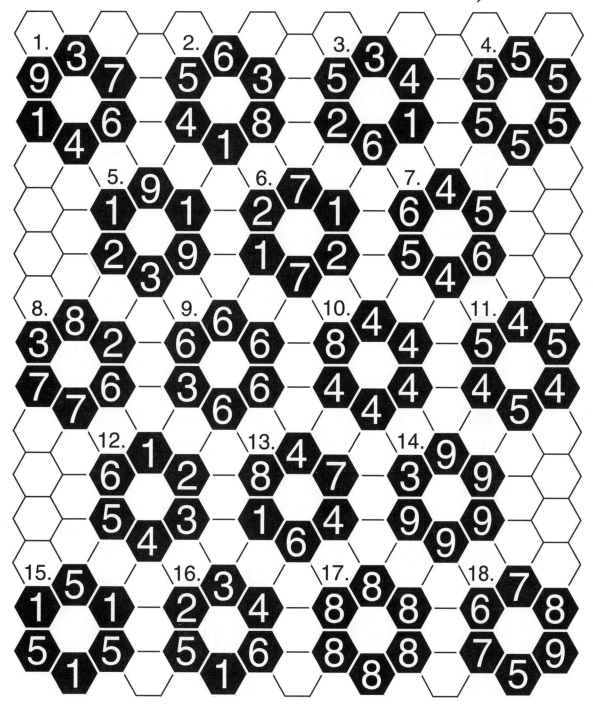

WHICH ONE DIFFERS?

In each problem, circle the one shape that is a bit different from the others.

1. a. b. c. d. e. f. g.

2. a. b. c. d. e. f. g.

3. a. b. c. d. e. f. g.

4. a. b. c. d. e. f. g.

5. a. b. c. d. e. f. g.

6. a. b. c. d. e. f. g.

7. a. b. c. d. e. f. g.

SUM STRINGS

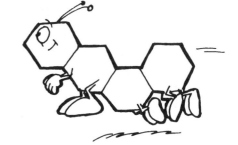

Make 16 different sum strings that total 15.

Fill in each set of four white hexagons with
four digits (1–9) that total 15. Don't use
the same set of four numbers more than once.

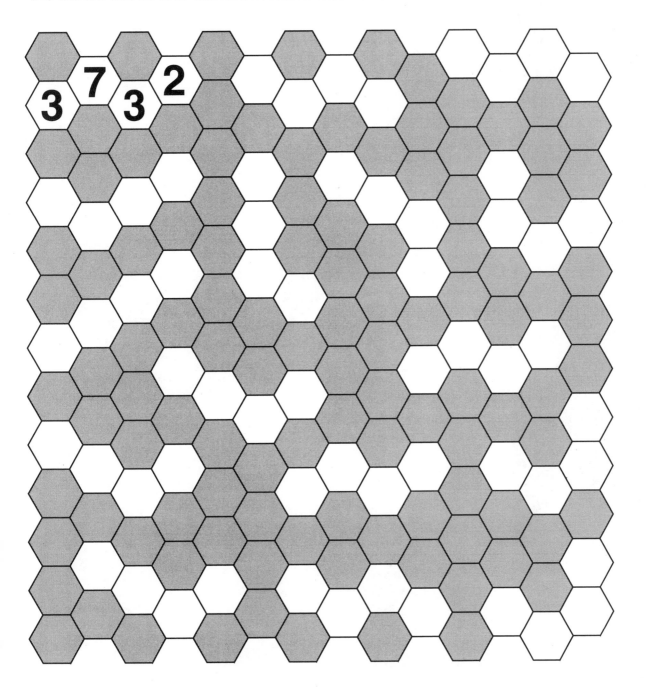

THE T PUZZLE

Have a copy of this page made. Cut out each of the four shapes below and place the pieces together in the shape of a T.

DATE DOINGS

Using the calendar at the right:

1. What day of the week is the 23rd?
   _____

2. What day of the week is the last day
   of the previous month? _____

3. If this month is July, what day of the
   week ends the month? _____

S	M	T	W	T	F	S
				9		

Using the calendar at the right:

4. What day of the week is the first of
   the month? _____

5. How many Thursdays are in this
   month, if it is February? _____

6. How many Thursdays are in this
   month, if it is January? _____

7. If it is June, what day will July 4th be? _____

S	M	T	W	T	F	S
		15				

Using the calendar at the right:

8. What month must this be?
   _____

9. Why does it have to be that month?
   _____

10. Is this calendar from a leap year?
    _____ Why? _____

11. Name a holiday that occurs in this month. _____

S	M	T	W	T	F	S
						7

NUMBER PATTERNS

Find each pattern.
Fill in the missing numbers.

1. | 7 | 17 | | | 47 | | | |

2. | | | 24 | 32 | | 48 | |

3. | 1 | 4 | | 16 | | | |

4. | | 135 | | | 150 | | |

5. | 12 | 23 | | | | 78 | |

6. | 1 | 8 | 27 | | | | |

7. | 08 | 17 | | 35 | | | 62 | |

8. | 64 | | 100 | | | | 225 |

9. | 1 | 1 | | 3 | 5 | | 13 | |

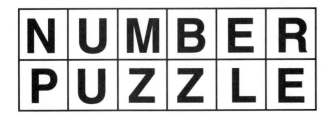

NUMBER PUZZLE

Use the "clues" below to write
the correct number in the squares.
(Don't write commas.)

[Puzzle grid with filled numbers:]
8 2 8 5
7
1
3

Across

1. Eight thousand two hundred eighty-five
5. Two hundred seventy-four thousand three hundred nine
7. One thousand four hundred fifteen
8. Nine hundred sixty-three
10. Two hundred seventy-three
11. Forty-three
12. Forty-eight
13. Six hundred twenty-nine
14. Two hundred fifty-three
16. Three thousand five hundred seventy-one
17. Two hundred seventy-eight thousand six hundred nine
19. Eight thousand one hundred

Down

1. Eight thousand seven hundred thirteen
2. Two hundred forty-five
3. Eighty-three
4. Five hundred nine
5. Two hundred forty-seven thousand eight hundred fifty-two
6. Nine hundred sixty-four thousand two hundred seventy-nine
7. One thousand two hundred forty-two
9. Three thousand three hundred ninety-one
13. Six thousand five hundred
15. Three hundred seventy-eight
16. Three hundred sixty
18. Eighty-one

Geometric designs in three kaleidoscopes

TARGET PRACTICE

Place three of the four given numbers
in the blanks to equal the target number.

1.

____ − ____ + ____ = 12

2.

____ + ____ − ____ = 0

3.

____ + ____ − ____ = 10

4.

____ − ____ + ____ = 8

5.

____ + ____ − ____ = 4

6.

____ − ____ + ____ = 3

7.

____ + ____ − ____ = 14

8.

____ − ____ + ____ = 2

DRAWING PATTERNS

Continue each drawing pattern.

1.

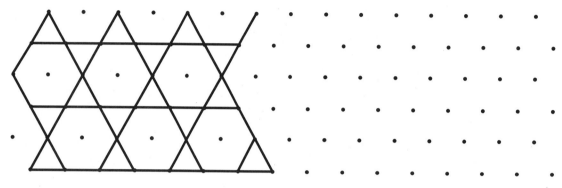

2.

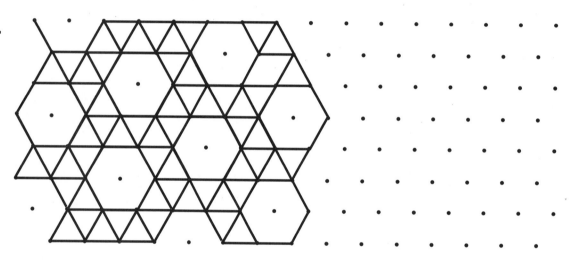

3.

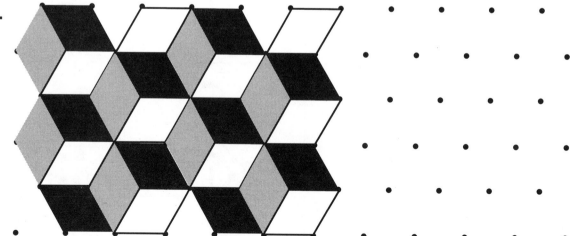

HOW BIG IS A MILLION?

1. If you laid a million one-dollar bills end-to-end, how far would they reach? First write down a wild guess. Then figure out the answer and see how close you were. (A dollar bill measures 6.14 inches.)

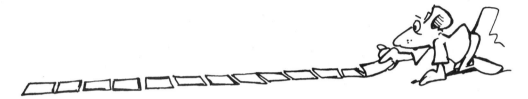

2. If a millionaire gave you one dollar every day, how many years would it take for him to give you a million dollars? (Assume there are no leap years.)

3. If you had a "super job" and earned $100 an hour, how many 40-hour weeks would you have to work to earn one million dollars?

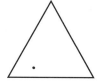  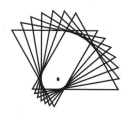

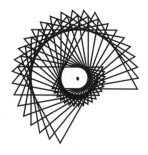 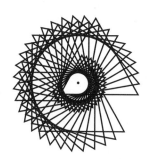 

 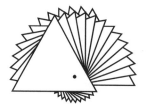 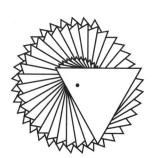

MULTIPLICATION MIX-UP

The table shown below is a "scrambled" multiplication table. The columns and the rows have been moved around to different positions. Use your knowledge of the multiplication facts and some good reasoning to fill in all the blank squares.

X	8				3				7
	12								
6			30						42
			25						
9				81				18	
	6			5			4		
					30				
	18		15			3			
4									
						32			

VISUAL THINKING

1. Find two designs that are exactly alike and in the same position.

a.   b.   c.   d.

e.   f.   g.   h.

i.   j.   k.   l.

2. What is each word?

a.

b.

c.

d.

3. Which two columns have the same five sets of circles?

a.

b.

c.

d.

SUM SHAPES

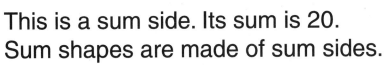

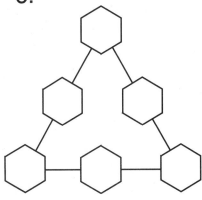

This is a sum side. Its sum is 20.
Sum shapes are made of sum sides.

In each problem below, use numbers
0, 1, 2, 3, 4, 5, 6, 7, 8 or 9 to make the sum. Don't
use the same number twice in one problem.

1.

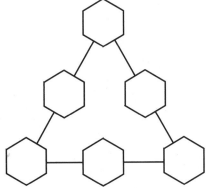

sum of 15
on each side

2.

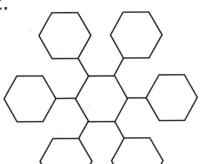

sum of 16
on each side

3.

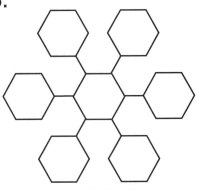

sum of 17
on each side

4.

sum of 15
on each side

5.

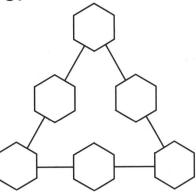

sum of 16
on each side

6.

sum of 17
on each side

Geometric Patterns in Quilts: Virginia Star

WHO AM I?

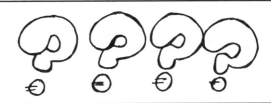

1. Five of me is six less than six of me.

Who am I?

2.  I am one less than twice the largest single-digit square number.

Who am I?

3. I am the largest three-digit number without using an 8, 9 or 5. By the way, none of my digits are the same.

Who am I?

4.  The sum of my two digits is nine. If my digits were reversed, I would be nine larger than I am.

Who am I?

5. My hundreds digit is twice my units digit. My units digit is one-fourth my tens digit. The product of my three digits contains one of my digits.

Who am I?

MAKING PAPER SNOWFLAKES

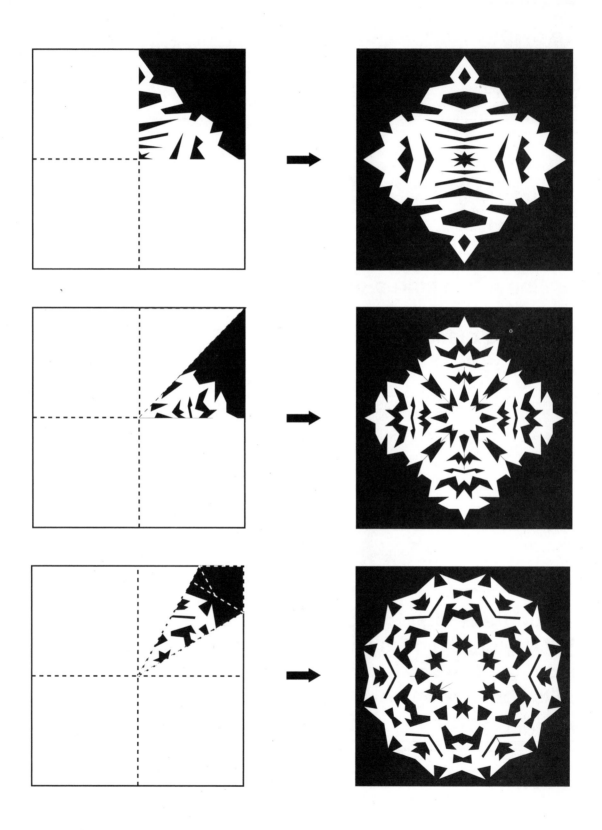

MAKING PAPER SNOWFLAKES

You can make paper snowflakes with just paper and scissors. Thinner paper is easier to cut. Colored paper or origami paper is great. Even facial tissue or paper towels will work.

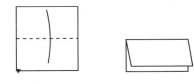

Step 1. If your paper isn't square, cut it to make it square.

Step 2. Fold the paper exactly in half.

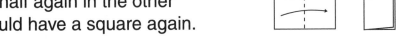

Step 3. Fold the paper in half again in the other direction. You should have a square again.

Step 4. Cut away pieces of paper from the small square. Cut from any of the four sides.

Step 5. When you have made all the cuts you want, open up the paper. You have a snowflake! Try another. You get better with practice.

If you'd like to make a snowflake whose four points are all alike (see the second example on the opposite page), fold your small square one more time diagonally and cut the three sides of the triangle.

To make a snowflake with six identical points, fold the small folded square into thirds. Cut the edges of the shape as before.

HOW MANY BLOCKS?

Count the number of blocks in each group.
Assume that blocks lie beneath other blocks
when they can't be seen, except for arches.
Groups 4, 5 and 6 would look the same if turned
halfway around.

1.

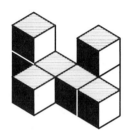

2.

3.

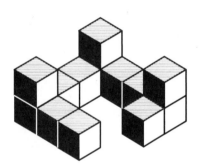

4.

5.

6.

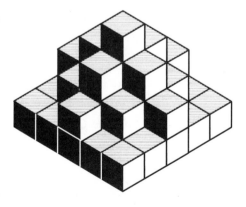

SUM STRINGS OF 16

Circle each sum string of at least 3 numbers that totals 16. Sum strings must be in a straight line in any direction.

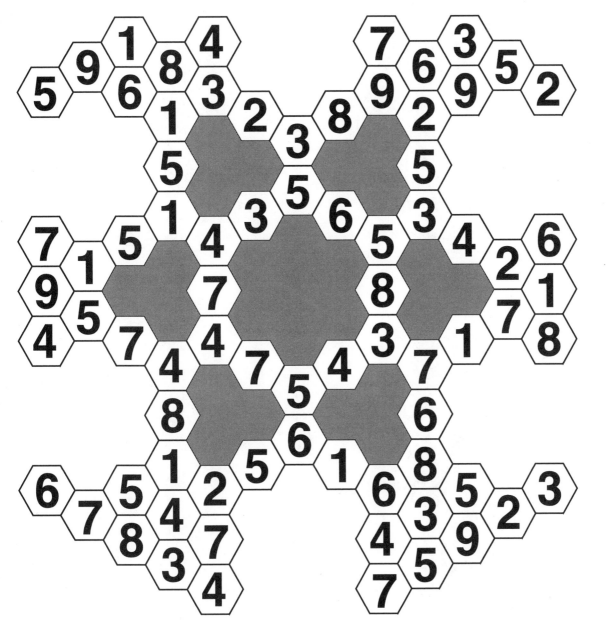

6 or more strings: Good
10 or more strings: Very Good
15 strings: Great!

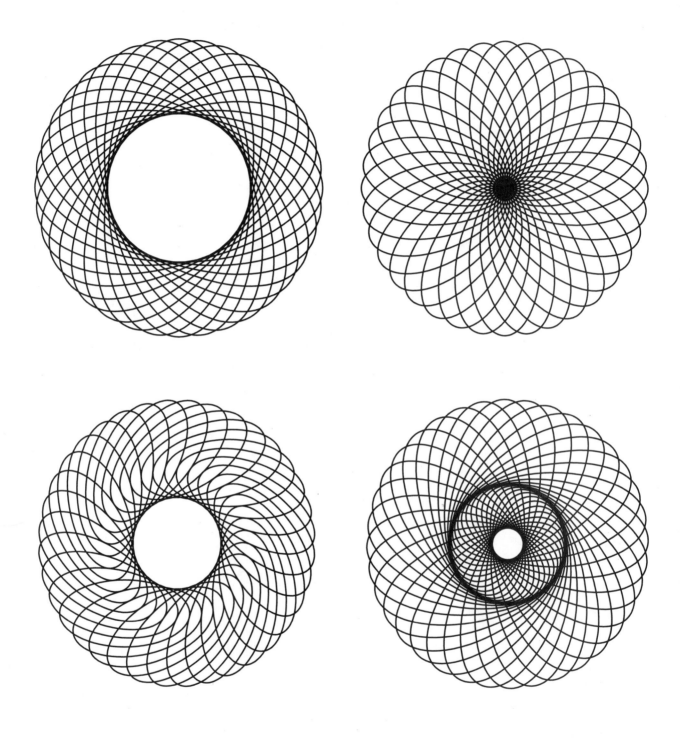

LARGEST – SMALLEST

Make the largest and smallest numbers,
using the numerals provided. Fill in each square.

1.
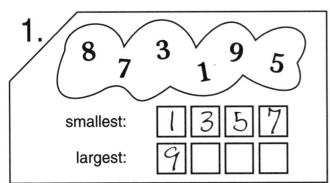

8 7 3 1 9 5

smallest: | 1 | 3 | 5 | 7 |

largest: | 9 | | | |

2.
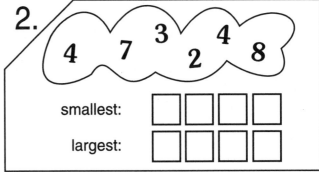

4 7 3 2 4 8

smallest: ☐ ☐ ☐ ☐

largest: ☐ ☐ ☐ ☐

3.
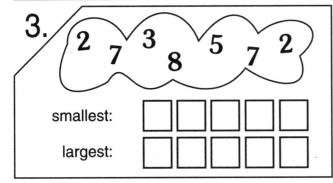

2 7 3 8 5 7 2

smallest: ☐ ☐ ☐ ☐ ☐

largest: ☐ ☐ ☐ ☐ ☐

4.
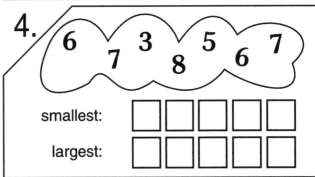

6 7 3 8 5 6 7

smallest: ☐ ☐ ☐ ☐ ☐

largest: ☐ ☐ ☐ ☐ ☐

5.
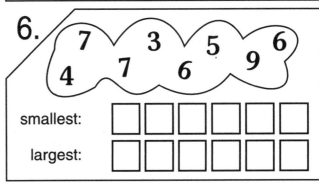

5 9 3 7 3 5 9 2

smallest: ☐ ☐ ☐ ☐ ☐ ☐

largest: ☐ ☐ ☐ ☐ ☐ ☐

6.

7 4 3 7 5 6 9 6

smallest: ☐ ☐ ☐ ☐ ☐ ☐

largest: ☐ ☐ ☐ ☐ ☐ ☐

7.
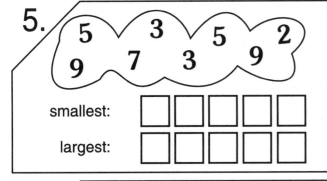

4 3 5 6 8 7 2 3 4 1

smallest: ☐ ☐ ☐ ☐ ☐ ☐

largest: ☐ ☐ ☐ ☐ ☐ ☐

8.
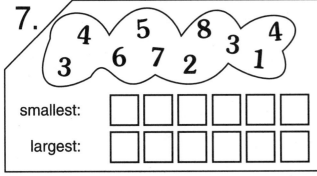

6 3 5 4 2 7 7 8 3 5

smallest: ☐ ☐ ☐ ☐ ☐ ☐

largest: ☐ ☐ ☐ ☐ ☐ ☐

SUM SHAPES

This is a sum side. Its sum is 13. Sum shapes are made of sum sides.

In each of the six problems below, use numbers 0, 1, 2, 3, 4, 5, 6, 7, 8 or 9 to make the sum. Don't use the same number twice in one problem.

1.

sum of
15 on
each side

2.

sum of
16 on
each side

3.

sum of
17 on
each side

4.

sum of
15 on
each side

5.

sum of
14 on
each side

6.

sum of
16 on
each side

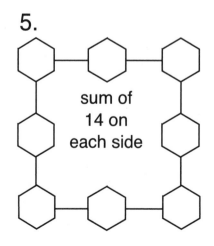
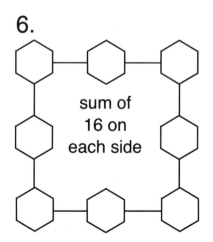

HOW MANY?

Count every one you can find.

1. How many triangles? 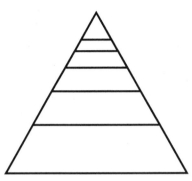	2. How many rectangles? A square is a rectangle. 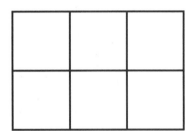
3. How many triangles? 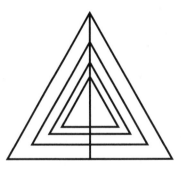	4. How many rectangles? 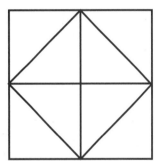
5. How many triangles? 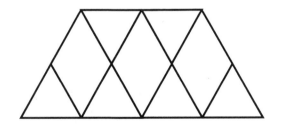	6. How many circles? 

Regular Polygons

A **polygon** is a closed figure whose sides are line segments. A **regular polygon** is one all of whose angles are congruent (equal) and all of whose sides are congruent (equal). Some polygon names are given below.

triangle	square	pentagon	hexagon
septagon or heptagon	octagon	nonagon	decagon
undecagon	dodecagon	13-gon	14-gon
15-gon	16-gon	17-gon	18-gon
19-gon	20-gon	100-gon	∎ ∎ ∎

NUMBER NAMES

Write each number name in words.

#	Number	Answer
1.	123	
2.	456	
3.	789	*seven hundred eighty-nine*
4.	500	
5.	203	
6.	87	
7.	444	
8.	2,021	
9.	32,404	
10.	1,020,099	

SAME SHAPES

In each problem, circle the two shapes that are exactly the same.

1.
a.	b.	c.	d.
e.	f.	g.	h.
i.	j.	k.	l.

2.
a.	b.	c.	d.
e.	f.	g.	h.
i.	j.	k.	l.

3.
a.	b.	c.	d.
e.	f.	g.	h.
i.	j.	k.	l.

4.
a.	b.	c.	d.
e.	f.	g.	h.
i.	j.	k.	l.

5.
a.	b.	c.	d.
e.	f.	g.	h.
i.	j.	k.	l.

6.
a.	b.	c.	d.
e.	f.	g.	h.
i.	j.	k.	l.

7.
a.	b.	c.	d.
e.	f.	g.	h.
i.	j.	k.	l.

8.
a.	b.	c.	d.
e.	f.	g.	h.
i.	j.	k.	l.

JUGGLING DIGITS

To solve certain problems, it is important to be able to make an organized list of digits.

1. List all the two-digit numbers that use only the digits 1, 2 or 3. It is OK to repeat a digit.

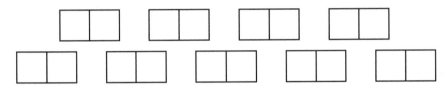

2. List all the three-digit numbers that use only the digits 2, 4, or 6. The number must contain a 2. Only the digit 2 may be used more than once in a number.

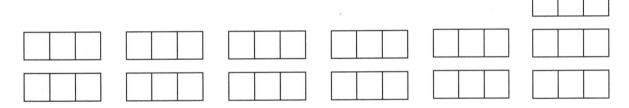

3. List all the four-digit numbers that use each of the digits 1, 3, 5 and 7 exactly once. Do not use other digits.

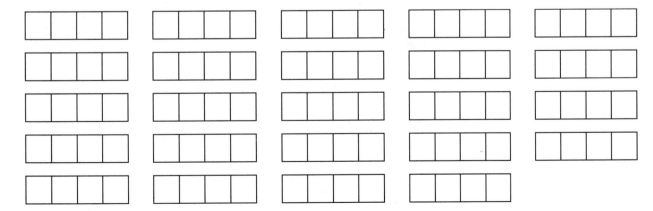

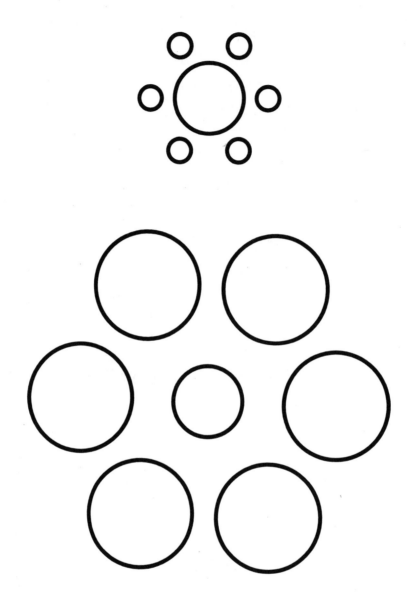

Which center circle appears larger?

TARGET PRACTICE

Place three of the four given numbers in the blanks to equal the target number. Write in the "+" and "−" signs.

1.

_____ _____ _____ = __0__

2.

_____ _____ _____ = __12__

3.

_____ _____ _____ = __10__

4.

_____ _____ _____ = __14__

5.

_____ _____ _____ = __6__

6.

_____ _____ _____ = __4__

7.

_____ _____ _____ = __2__

8.

_____ _____ _____ = __7__

SCALE DRAWING
SCALE DRAWING
SCALE DRAWING
SCALE DRAWING
SCALE DRAWING

Sometimes artists make a very large drawing or painting by copying a smaller drawing. They locate their position in the drawing by using a grid. Can you copy the small drawing onto the larger grid?

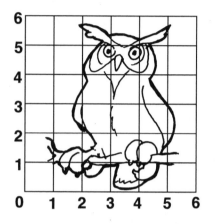

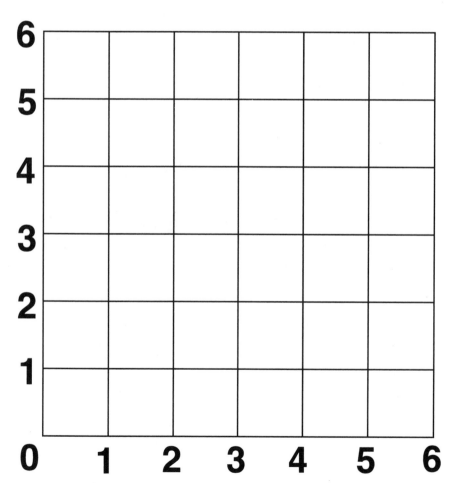

PROBLEMS TO SOLVE

1. Write all the three-digit numbers possible using the digits 4, 5, 6 and 7. (Use each digit only once in a number.)

2. Judy's rubber ball bounces exactly half the height from which it falls. She drops the ball from the top of a building 64 meters tall.

   How high will the ball bounce on its eighth bounce? _____

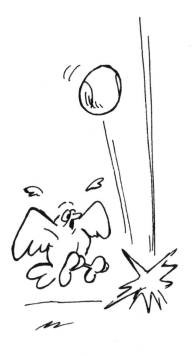

3. Four classmates were all born in the same month. Ann is one week older than Bill. Chuck is two days younger than Bill. Dana is both taller and older than Chuck. Dana is four days older than Bill.

   Who is the youngest? _____
   Who is the oldest? _____

GEOMETRIC PATTERNS

PUZZLE PIECES

1. Which two lettered pieces are not part of the design?

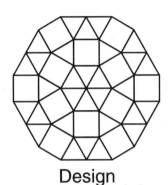

Design

 a.

b.

c.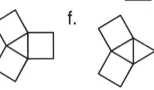

d.

e.

f.

2. Which two lettered pieces do not belong to the puzzle?

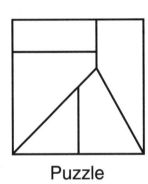

Puzzle

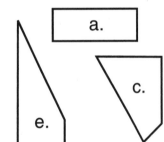

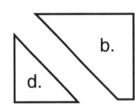

3. Find two identical shapes.

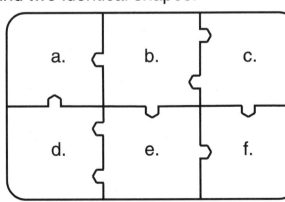

STRAIGHT-LINE CURVES

You can draw a circle by drawing all straight lines. Here's how. Use a ruler with a straight edge. Connect the two 1's, the two 2's, the two 3's, and so on. Push down on the ruler so it doesn't slip.

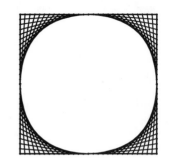

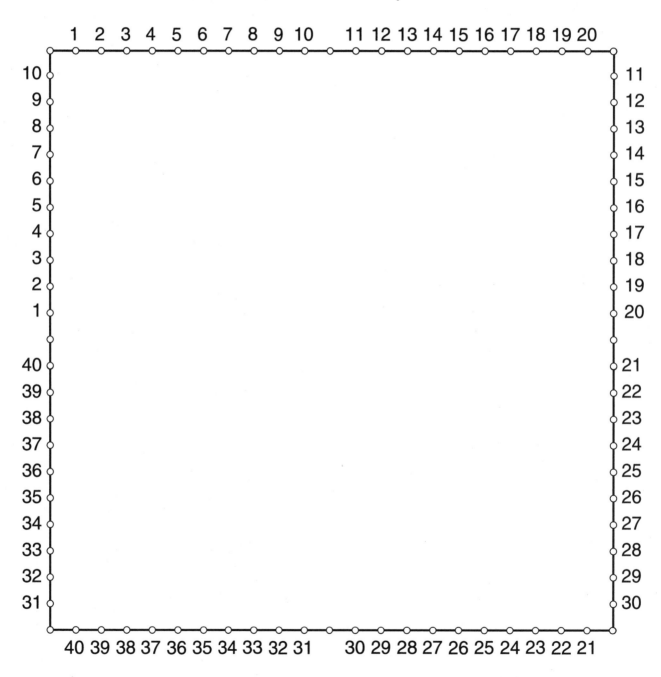

YOU GRADE IT

How did Bobbie Marks do on this test? Place a **C** by each correct answer. Place a check ✔ by each wrong answer and write in the correct answer.

Computation Test

<u>Bobbie Marks</u>
name

1. 504
  − 276
  218

2. 34
  59
  23
  + 78
  194

3. 287
  x 4
  1248

4. $ 5.75
  3.37
  + 6.25
  15.37

5. 6,572
  834
  + 8,209
  15,615

6. 435 + 0.7 + 2.65
  435
  0.7
  2.65
  437.35

7. $ 45 − 13.75
  $45.00
  13.75
  $31.25

8. 300 x 20 x 200
  300
  20
  60000
  200
  12,000,000

9. Write in standard form:

sixty-three billion one hundred thirty-seven million eight hundred twenty-four thousand five

63,137,824,500

CROSSNUMBER PUZZLE

Fill in the squares with numbers.

Across

1. Yards in a mile

5. Tablespoons in two cups

7. Nickels in $8.95

9. 288 ÷ 6

10. Six dozen

11. Nineteen squared

12. Ounces in a pound

13. Pounds in a ton

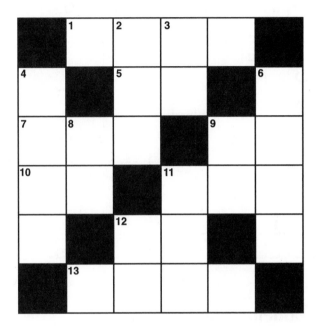

Down

2. 1267 – 528

3. Two less than eight squared

4. 18 × 343

6. 20% of 14,050

8. Half a gross

9. 2944 ÷ 64

11. Degrees in one complete rotation

12. Number of centimeters in a decimeter

EVEN AND ODD NUMBER PATTERNS

Fill in the blank squares below, using **E** for an even number and **O** for an odd number.

Even-Odd Addition

+	0	1	2	3	4	5	6	7	8	9
0	E	O								
1	O	E								
2										
3										
4										
5										
6										
7										
8										
9										

Even-Odd Multiplication

X	0	1	2	3	4	5	6	7	8	9
0	E	E								
1	E	O								
2										
3										
4										
5										
6										
7										
8										
9										

Addition Conclusions

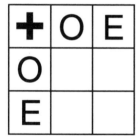

+	O	E
O		
E		

Multiplication Conclusions

X	O	E
O		
E		

Now, use the patterns from the charts you completed above to make some conclusions in the lower boxes.

SUM STRINGS

Circle each horizontal or vertical string
of three numbers that total 17.

```
        7                           5
    2  4  5  8           7  7  3  9
  5     3  9  4  6     8  4  1  6        4
6  4  8        1           5           1  7  2
  9  7     7  5  6  8  1  8  6  2     8  9
  4  8  6  2     4  7  3  6        8  6  5  6
     1     9  9     5  9        1  6     3
           7  4  5        3  9  5
           6  6  1        7  4  9
     1     4  8     6  2     2  4     9
  8  9  2  3     4  3  8  5     9  8  7  4
  6  3     1  6  8  7  2  4  1  3     1  6
6  2  9        5           8        5  3  8
  7     1  7  8  5     7  6  2  4     7
     5  7  5  6           3  9  8  3
        8                       7
```

five-hole sand dollar

chambered nautilus

bat starfish

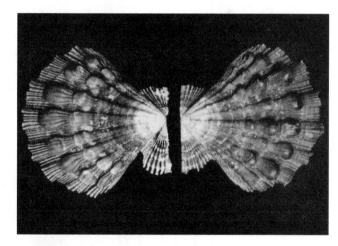

lion's paw scallop

marlinspike

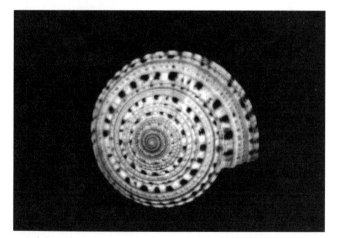

sundial

Photo source: Amy Lyn Edwards

SAME SHAPES

Which pairs are exactly the same?

Triangles: _____ and _____
_____ and _____

Squares: _____ and _____
Parallelograms: _____ and _____
Rectangles (that aren't squares): _____ and _____

1.	2.	3.	4.	5.
6.	7.	8.	9.	10.
11.	12.	13.	14.	15.
16.	17.	18.	19.	20.
21.	22.	23.	24.	25.
26.	27.	28.	29.	30.

SUM SHORTCUTS

Multiplication is a shortcut for addition.
Use multiplication to find these sums:

1. 17
    17
    17
    17
    17
    17
    +17
    ———

2. 24
    24
    24
    24
    24
    24
    +25
    ———

3. 16 + 14 + 16 + 14 + 16 + 14 =

4. How many gummed labels on the four sheets?

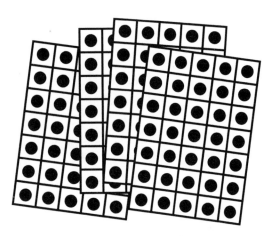

5. How many stamps?

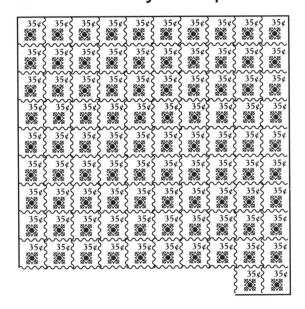

6. How many small squares?

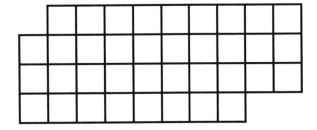

7. What is the total value of these stamps?

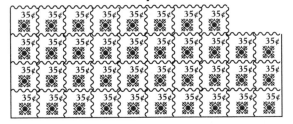

PROBLEMS TO SOLVE

1. A jeweler has four small bars that are supposed to be gold. He knows that one is counterfeit. The counterfeit bar has a slightly different weight from the real gold bar. Using only a balance scale, how can the jeweler find the counterfeit bar?

2. The Tigers played 14 soccer games. They won eight more games than they lost. What was their win-loss record?
_____ wins and _____ losses

3. How many different rectangles are in this figure? (A square is considered a rectangle.)

HEXAGON PUZZLE

Have a copy of this page made. Cut out each of the five shapes below and place the pieces together in the shape of a regular hexagon. (All 6 sides are equal, and all 6 angles are equal.)

TARGET PRACTICE

Place the three numbers in the
blanks to equal the target number.

1.

___ x ___ + ___ = <u>15</u>

2.

___ x ___ + ___ = <u>12</u>

3.

___ x ___ + ___ = <u>20</u>

4.

___ x ___ – ___ = <u>9</u>

5.

___ x ___ – ___ = <u>16</u>

6.

___ x ___ – ___ = <u>0</u>

7.

___ x ___ + ___ = <u>25</u>

8.

___ x ___ – ___ = <u>25</u>

DRAWING PATTERNS

Continue each drawing pattern.

1.

2.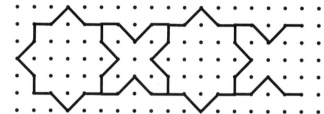

3.

4.

WHO AM I?

1. I am less than 10. If I were doubled, I would be 15 less than my square.

   Who am I?

2. 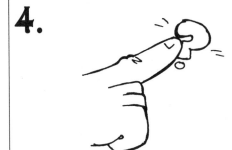 The sum of my two digits is 15. The product of my digits is 31 less than I am.

   Who am I?

3. My square contains both of my digits. I am less than 25 but more than zero.

   Who am I?

4.  I am a three-digit number. Place your finger over my units digit and you see a square number. The sum of my digits is 18. Only one of my digits is greater than five.

   Who am I?

5. Like my friend above, I am a three-digit whole number, and the sum of my digits is 18. If I were four more, the sum of my digits would be four. Each of my digits is either a square or a cube.

   Who am I?

What Can You Do with an R?

You can:

R keep it	**R** shrink it	**R** enlarge it	**R** stretch it	**R** smash it	**R** halve it
F halve it	**R** tilt it	**Я** reverse it	**R** eat it	**P** slice it	**⊚R** register it
Rᴿ follow it	**R** outline it	**R** shadow it	**ЯR** reflect it	**r** lowercase it	**B** bend it

Or you can:

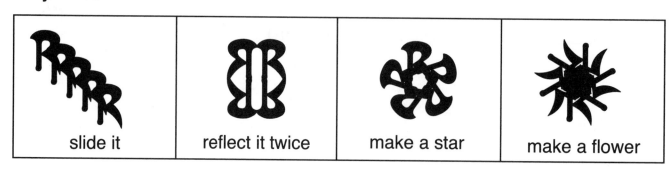

slide it   reflect it twice   make a star   make a flower

Or you can even make some designs:

HOW MANY?

Count *every* one you can find.

1. How many triangles?	2. How many rectangles?
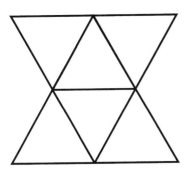	

3. How many hexagons?	4. How many circles?
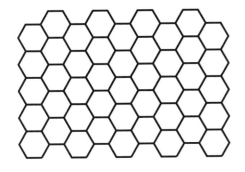	
Did multiplication help you?	

5. How many triangles?	6. How many rectangles?
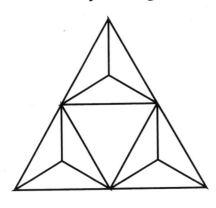	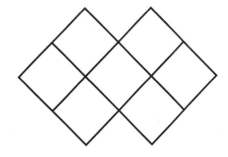

TALL TALES

Drawing a sketch or crossing out possibilities often helps solve a problem.

Together, the four clues below reveal the relative height of four boys. Each clue reveals part of the answer. Cross out initials under the four drawings as you discover who doesn't fit each place. The results revealed by the first clue are already crossed out.

Clues

1. Les is taller than Dave.

2. Les is taller than Ken.

3. Dave is taller than Ken.

4. Jeff is taller than Les.

What the Clue Reveals

So, Dave can't be the tallest, and Les can't be the _____.
(Those letters are crossed out under the drawing.)

So, Ken can't be the _____ and, therefore, Les can't be the second shortest. (Cross out letters.)

So, Dave can't be the _____, and Ken is shorter than two boys. (Cross out letters.)

Les can't be the tallest, so _____ is tallest. (Cross out the remaining possibilities. Now you've solved the puzzle.)

Answer: _____, _____, _____, _____
       tallest   shortest

BEING OBSERVANT

What do we have in common?

More than one answer may be correct.

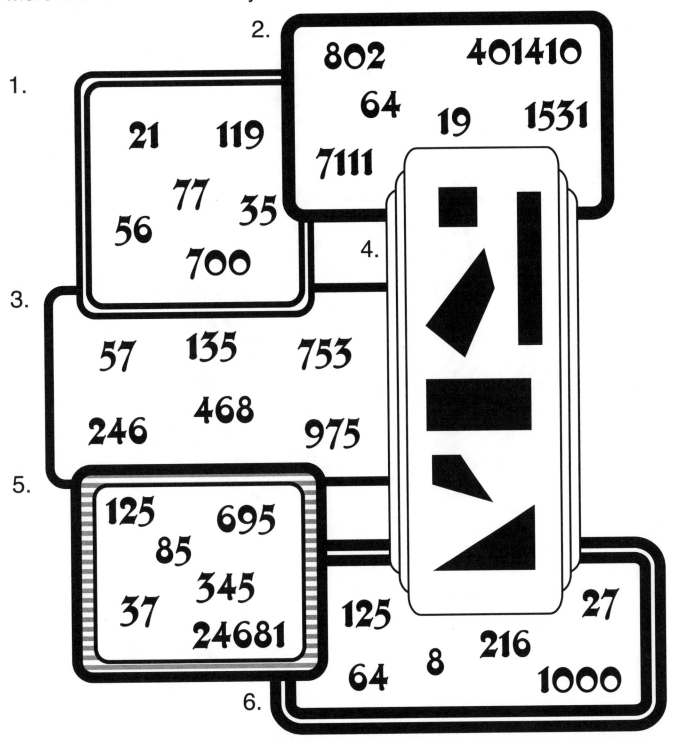

1.

21   119

77

56   35

700

2.

802   401410

64   19   1531

7111

3.

57   135   753

468

246   975

5.

125   695

85

37   345

24681

6.

125   27

8   216

64   1000

Rotate this page in a circular motion.

PROBLEMS TO SOLVE

1. Nancy is Barb's sister. Annette is Nancy's daughter. Kay is Annette's sister. If Kate is Barb's daughter, what relation is:

   - Nancy to Kay? _____
   - Kay to Barb? _____
   - Barb to Annette? _____
   - Kate to Annette? _____

2. A teacher asked each member of the class to write his or her favorite number less than 10 on a slip of paper.

   - No one wrote zero, two, five, or nine.
   - Ten students chose odd numbers.
   - Ten students chose even numbers
   - Numbers three and seven tied for second with four votes each.
   - Number seven got more votes than number six.
   - Numbers greater than five received more votes than numbers less than five.

   What was the most popular number in this class? _____

HOW MANY?

Count *every* one you can find.

... 17,18

1. How many squares? How many rectangles? 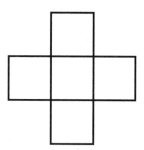	2. How many rectangles? 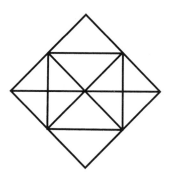
3. How many rectangles? How many triangles? 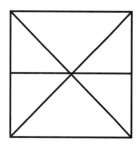	4. How many regular pentagons? How many triangles? 
5. How many squares? How many triangles? 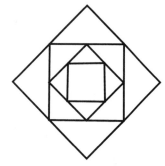	6. How many rectangles? How many triangles? 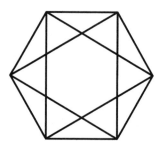

GROUPING NUMBERS

Parentheses say,

"Do Me First."

$(4 \times 5) - 1 = 19$

$4 \times (5 - 1) = 16$

Insert parentheses where needed to make each number sentence true.

1. $3 + 3 \times 2 = 12$	2. $3 + 3 \times 2 = 9$
3. $8 \div 2 - 1 = 8$	4. $8 \div 2 - 1 = 3$
5. $15 - 7 - 2 = 6$	6. $15 - 7 - 2 = 10$
7. $3 \times 5 - 2 = 13$	8. $3 \times 5 - 2 = 9$
9. $2 \times 6 + 5 = 17$	10. $2 \times 6 + 5 = 22$
11. $4 \div 2 \times 2 = 4$	12. $4 \div 2 \times 2 = 1$

GEOMETRIC PATTERNS

RACE RESULTS

Here are some thinking problems about races. It may help to draw some pictures on scratch paper.

1. Three girls ran.
Sara wasn't first.
Jane wasn't last.
Margo beat Jane.

Who came in first?
Who came in second?

2. Four horses ran.
#2 beat #1.
#4 beat #1.
#3 beat #4.
#2 lost to #4.

Who won?
Who was second?

3. Five dogs raced.
Fido came in third.
Tippy beat Fido.
Red beat Tippy.

Who won the race?

MATCHSTICK PUZZLES

1. Which two matches could be moved to form four equilateral triangles?

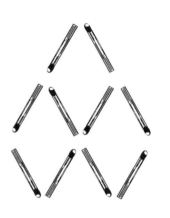

2. Move one stick to make two houses.

3. Remove three matches to leave three squares.

VISUAL FRACTIONS

Write the fractions that tell what part of
each shape is black and what part is white.
Write each fraction in lowest terms.

1.	2.	3.	4.
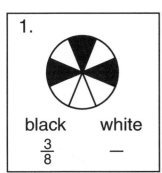	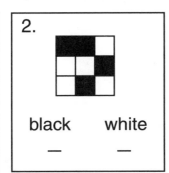	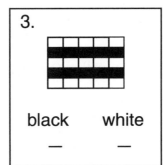	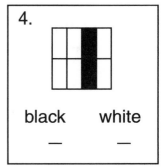
black white	black white	black white	black white
$\frac{3}{8}$ ___	___ ___	___ ___	___ ___

5.	6.	7.	8.
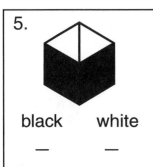	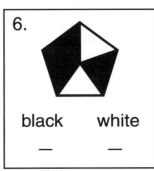	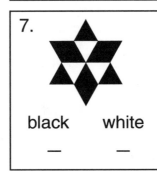	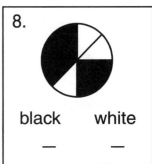
black white	black white	black white	black white
___ ___	___ ___	___ ___	___ ___

Shade in the fractional part that is given.

9.	10.	11.	12.
$\frac{2}{5}$ 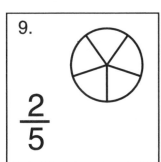	$\frac{5}{12}$ 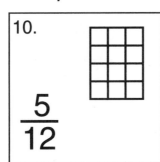	$\frac{3}{7}$ 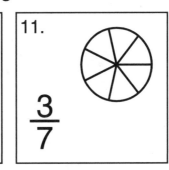	$\frac{5}{9}$ 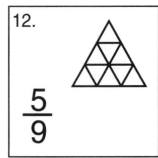

13.	14.	15.	16.
$\frac{7}{12}$ 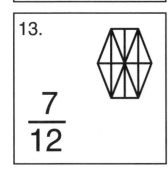	$\frac{1}{3}$ 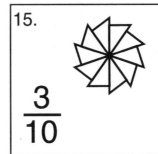	$\frac{3}{10}$ 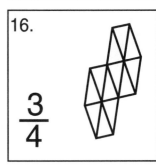	$\frac{3}{4}$ 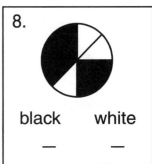

LOGOS

Logos are designs that identify a product or company. Logos are often geometric. Designers frequently design logos to be simple and symmetrical. Sometimes the company's initials or their products are in the logo.

Here are some examples of typical logos.

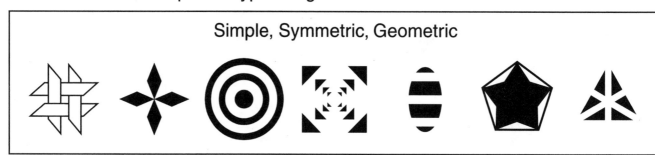

Simple, Symmetric, Geometric

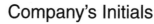

Company's Initials

Company's Product

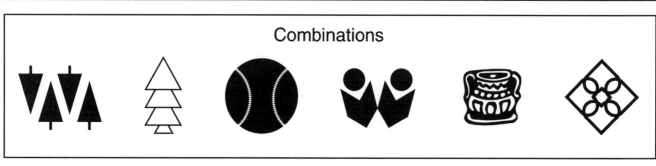

Combinations

Look through newspapers and magazines to find 10 good examples of the properties shown above. Design a logo of your own.

WHAT FRACTIONAL PART?

Using the square below, which has dividing lines drawn, figure what fraction of each problem is black. Write your answer in lowest terms.

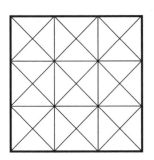

1. _____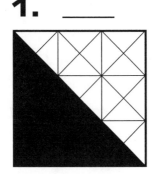

2. _____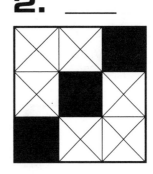

3. _____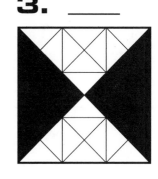

4. _____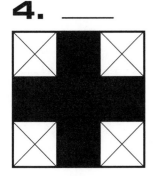

5. _____

6. _____

7. _____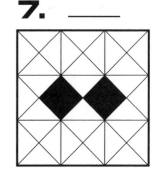

8. _____

9. _____

10. _____

11. _____

VERTICAL SYMMETRY

Vertical lines are lines that go straight up and down. *Horizontal* lines go sideways. If you place a mirror to the side of an alphabet letter, it may look the same in the mirror or it may look different. If it looks the same, we say it has *vertical symmetry.*

The letters below have been reflected (flipped) across a vertical line. The vertical lines are called *axes of symmetry.* Those letters that look the same on both sides of the line have vertical symmetry. If the letters don't look the same, then they don't have vertical symmetry. The letter A has vertical symmetry in the alphabet on the left side of the page. The letter B does not have vertical symmetry.

1. Circle all the letters in each alphabet that have vertical symmetry.
2. The words at the right have vertical symmetry. List some more.

HORIZONTAL SYMMETRY

Horizontal lines are lines that go across or lines that are level with the horizon. Vertical lines go up and down. If you place a mirror below or above an alphabet letter, it may look the same in the mirror or it may look different. If it looks the same, we say it has *horizontal symmetry.*

The dark letters below have been reflected (flipped) across a horizontal line.

A B C D E F G H I J K L M N O P Q R S T U V W X Y Z
_____
∀ B C D E Ⅎ G H I ⅃ K ⌐ M N O ᑫ Ꝺ Я S ⊥ ∩ Λ Ɯ X Y Z

Those letters that look the same have horizontal symmetry. If the letters don't look the same, then they don't have horizontal symmetry. The letter A has vertical symmetry but not horizontal symmetry. The letter C has horizontal symmetry but not vertical symmetry.

1. Circle all the letters in the alphabet above that have horizontal symmetry.
2. The words below have horizontal symmetry. List some more.

CHECK   **HI**   **DOE**
_____
CHECK   **HI**   **DOE**

The horizontal lines on this page are called *axes of symmetry.*

Immortality by John Robinson
Used by permission of Edition Limitée.

A GOOD TURN

Rotate means to turn about a point. The flag below is shown rotated one-fifth of a complete turn in each step.

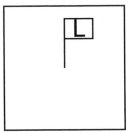 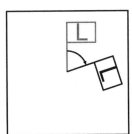 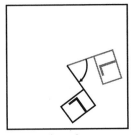 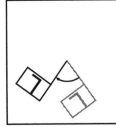 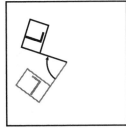

| 1. Starting position | 2. 1/5 of a complete rotation | 3. 1/5 of a complete rotation | 4. 1/5 of a complete rotation | 5. 1/5 of a complete rotation |

Here is a square rotated one-fifth of a complete rotation about one of its corners.

    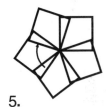

1.   2.   3.   4.   5.

Shown below are designs created by rotating a square about one of its corners.

6 rotations   8 rotations   9 rotations   12 rotations   20 rotations

Beautiful geometric designs often contain shapes that have been rotated. Can you find some? Can you make some?

WHEEL OF FRACTION

For each box, find the fractional part of a circle that corresponds with the fraction below the box. Place the letter of that fractional part in the box. What is the hidden message?

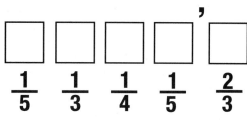

$$\frac{1}{5} \quad \frac{1}{3} \quad \frac{1}{4} \quad \frac{1}{5} \quad \frac{2}{3} \qquad \frac{5}{6} \quad \frac{3}{4} \quad \frac{3}{4} \quad \frac{2}{5}$$

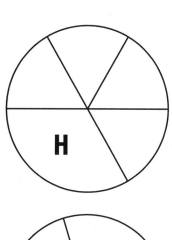

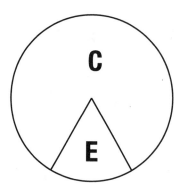

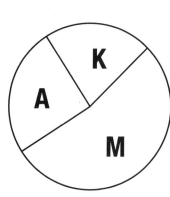

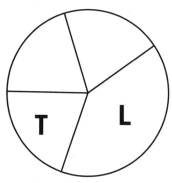

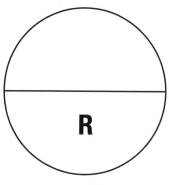

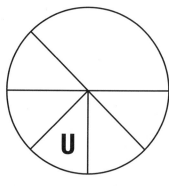

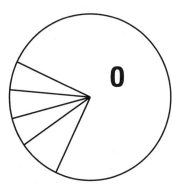

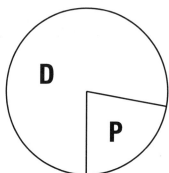

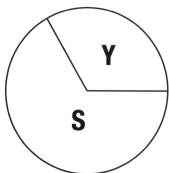

POLYOMINOES

Polyominoes are shapes made from squares. Here are some polyomino names:

Monomino
(1 square)

Domino
(2 squares)

Tromino
(3 squares)

Tetromino
(4 squares)

The following shapes **are not** polyominoes. In a polyomino, squares must share an edge.

There are **five different** tetrominoes. Tetrominoes are made of four squares. Can you draw all five on the square grids below? (The same shape turned in a different direction is not different.)

STAR DESIGNS

CREATING A DESIGN

The steps below show how a designer makes a five-pointed star.

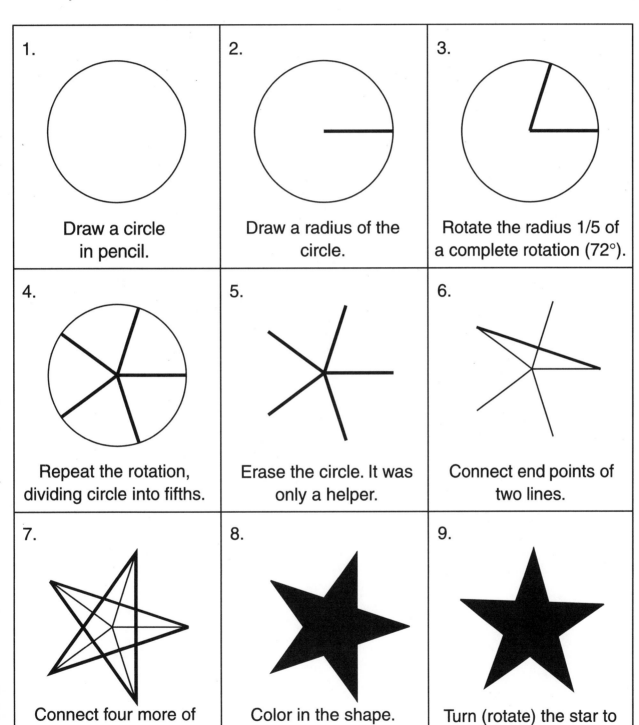

1. Draw a circle in pencil.

2. Draw a radius of the circle.

3. Rotate the radius 1/5 of a complete rotation (72°).

4. Repeat the rotation, dividing circle into fifths.

5. Erase the circle. It was only a helper.

6. Connect end points of two lines.

7. Connect four more of those lines.

8. Color in the shape.

9. Turn (rotate) the star to point straight up.

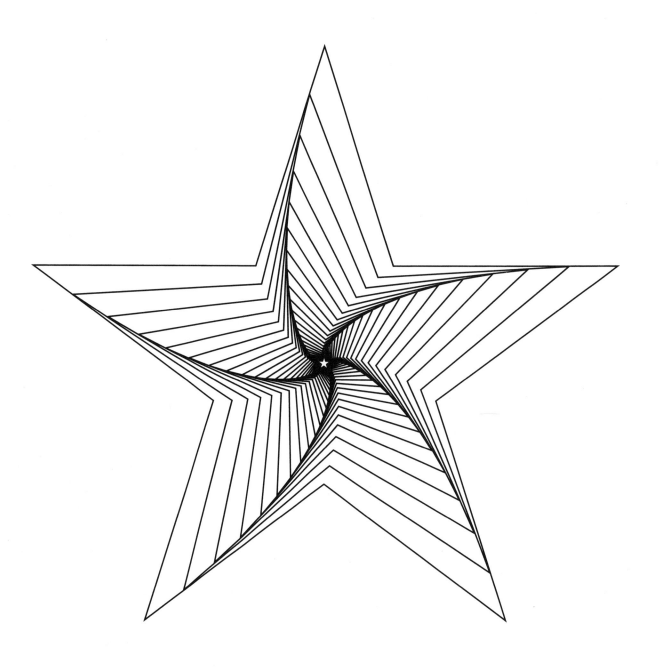

TARGET PRACTICE

Insert parentheses where needed to make each number sentence true. Remember, what's inside parentheses is done first.

1.  8 − 6 x 7 = 14	**2.**  9 x 6 + 4 = 90
3.  5 + 2 x 6 = 17	**4.**  4 x 9 − 6 = 12
5.  5 + 6 x 2 = 22	**6.**  9 − 8 x 3 = 3
7.  9 − 6 ÷ 2 = 6	**8.**  8 x 3 + 1 = 32

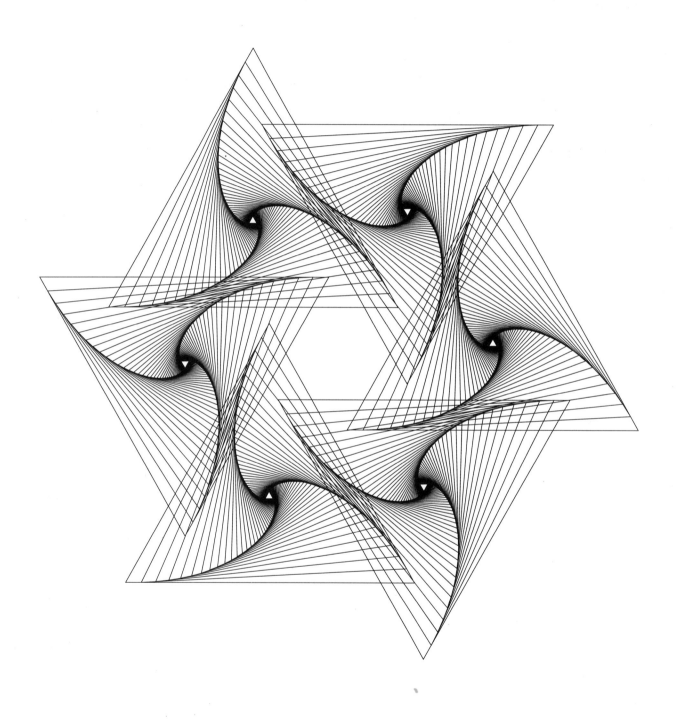

RELATIONSHIPS

Fill in the blank to make each sentence true.

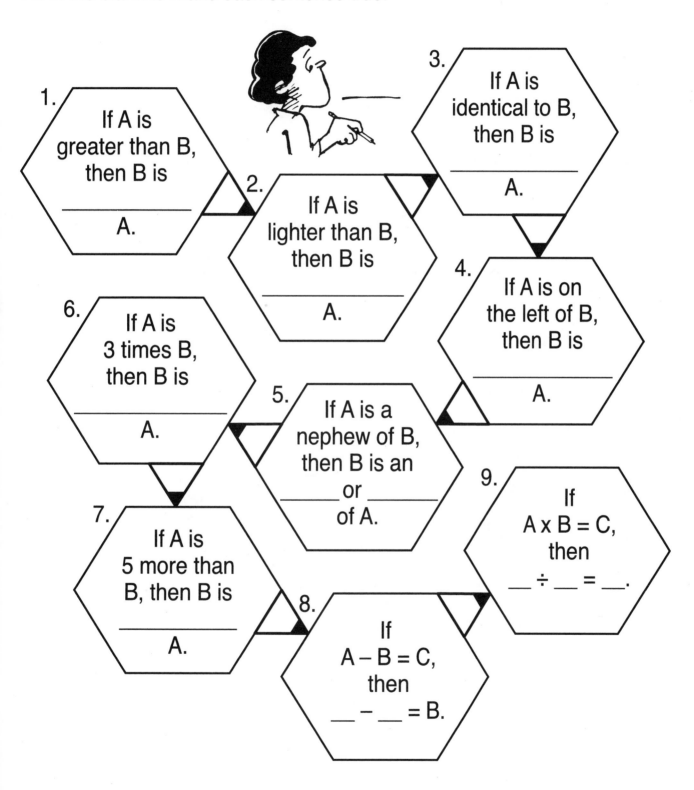

1. If A is greater than B, then B is _____ A.

2. If A is lighter than B, then B is _____ A.

3. If A is identical to B, then B is _____ A.

4. If A is on the left of B, then B is _____ A.

5. If A is a nephew of B, then B is an _____ or _____ of A.

6. If A is 3 times B, then B is _____ A.

7. If A is 5 more than B, then B is _____ A.

8. If A – B = C, then ___ – ___ = B.

9. If A x B = C, then ___ ÷ ___ = ___.

LOGIC LOOPS

Write at least one number, **if possible,** in each of the seven sections in each problem.

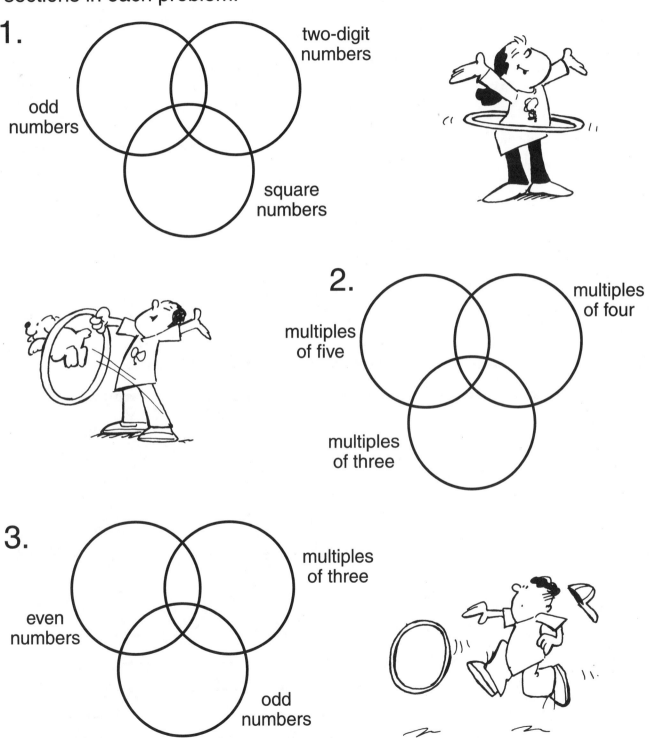

1.

two-digit numbers

odd numbers

square numbers

2.

multiples of five

multiples of four

multiples of three

3.

even numbers

multiples of three

odd numbers

GEOMETRIC PATTERNS

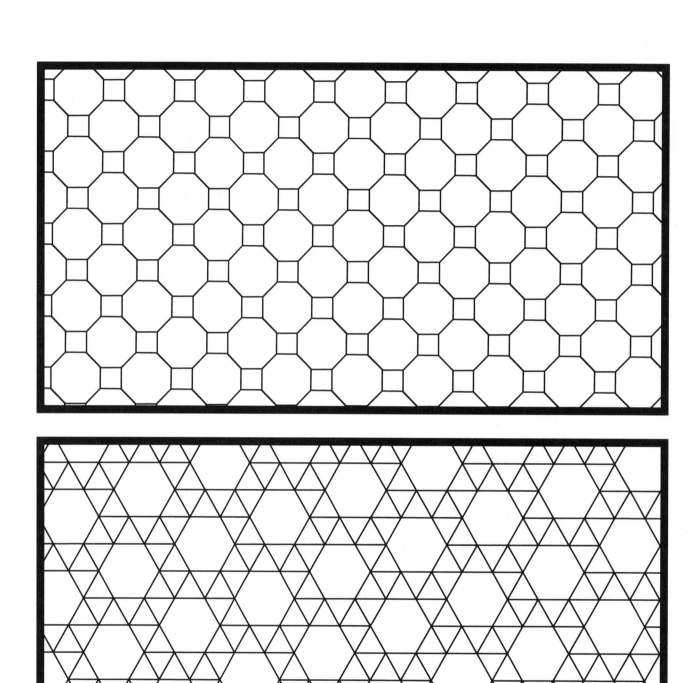

WHAT DIRECTION?

Do you know the general location of major cities in the United States? Maps usually have a direction locator indicating north. Sometimes they have a more elaborate locator like the one shown below. This locator is like a circular protractor or a magnetic compass.

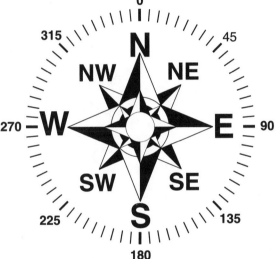

Kansas City is located south and west of Chicago. We say that Kansas City is southwest of Chicago. Chicago is located northeast of Kansas City. St. Louis is considered east of Denver, since it is closer to east than it is to southeast.

Give the most accurate directions:

1. Salt Lake City is _____ of Seattle.
2. San Francisco is _____ of San Diego.
3. New York is _____ of Chicago.
4. San Francisco is _____ of St. Louis.
5. New Orleans is _____ of Dallas.
6. Seattle is _____ of San Francisco.
7. Atlanta is _____ of New Orleans.
8. Denver is _____ of Dallas.

Ephesus, Turkey

Pearl Mosque, Delhi, India

Mexico City, Mexico

Beijing, China

Hangzhou, China

Western Expansion Memorial Arch, St. Louis, Missouri

All photos except lower right: Christine Freeman
Lower right photo: Dale Seymour

TRY TILING

You could tile the floor with these shapes made of six triangles.
Continue each of the patterns below. Try your own on grid paper.

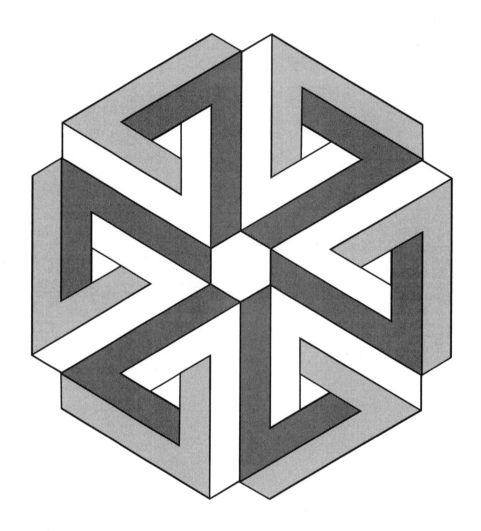

ONE TOUGH PUZZLE

You will need to have a system and be well organized to get all of the answers right to the questions below. Good luck!

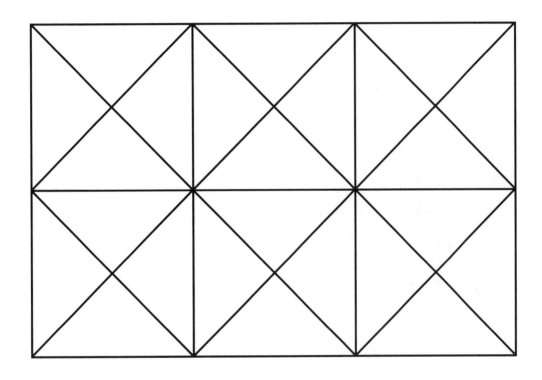

1. How many rectangles that aren't squares? _____

2. How many triangles? _____

3. How many squares? _____

4. How many parallelograms? _____

Remember, a square is both a rectangle and a parallelogram.

Resources

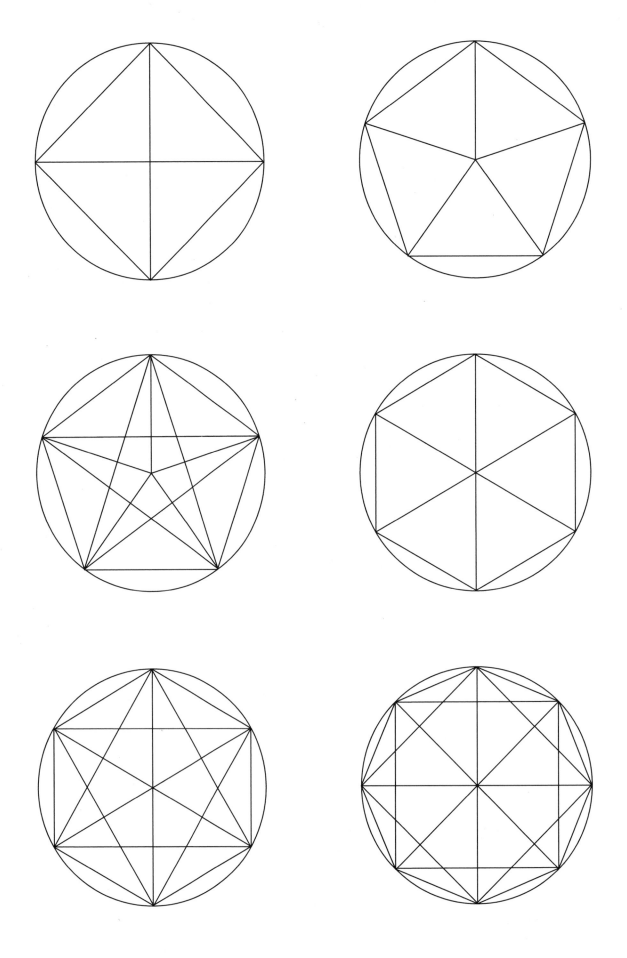

Smart Answers

1 Tic-Tac-Number

1.
1	8	6
7	5	3
2	9	4

2.
1	0	3
2	8	4
7	6	5

2 Black or White Arrows?
You should see both. Which did you see first?

3 Sum Rings
1. 30
2. 27
3. 21
4. 30
5. 25
6. 20
7. 30
8. 33
9. 33
10. 28
11. 27
12. 21
13. 30
14. 48
15. 18
16. 21
17. 48
18. 42

4 Which One Differs?
1. f
2. a
3. g
4. e
5. b
6. f
7. e

5 Sum Strings
There are 23 possible combinations:

1149	1266	2229	2355
1158	1338	2238	2445
1167	1347	2247	3336
1239	1356	2256	3345
1248	1446	2337	3444
1257	1455	2346	

6 The T Puzzle

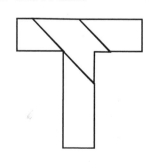

7 Date Doings
1. Thursday
2. Tuesday
3. Friday
4. Wednesday
5. Four
6. Five
7. Monday
8. February
9. Only 28 days are displayed.
10. No. There is no space for February 29th.
11. Valentine's Day or Presidents' Day

8 Number Patterns

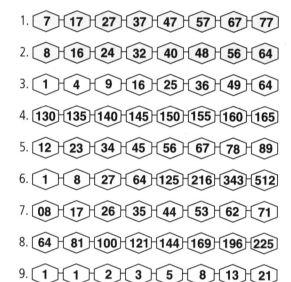

1. 7 – 17 – 27 – 37 – 47 – 57 – 67 – 77
2. 8 – 16 – 24 – 32 – 40 – 48 – 56 – 64
3. 1 – 4 – 9 – 16 – 25 – 36 – 49 – 64
4. 130 – 135 – 140 – 145 – 150 – 155 – 160 – 165
5. 12 – 23 – 34 – 45 – 56 – 67 – 78 – 89
6. 1 – 8 – 27 – 64 – 125 – 216 – 343 – 512
7. 08 – 17 – 26 – 35 – 44 – 53 – 62 – 71
8. 64 – 81 – 100 – 121 – 144 – 169 – 196 – 225
9. 1 – 1 – 2 – 3 – 5 – 8 – 13 – 21

9 Number Puzzle

		8	2	8	5	
	2	7	4	3	0	9
1	4	1	5		9	6	3
2	7	3			4	3
4	8			6	2	9
2	5	3		3	5	7	1
	2	7	8	6	0	9
		8	1	0	0	

11 Target Practice

Answers may vary but may include:

1. $7 - 1 + 6 = 12$
2. $6 + 1 - 7 = 0$
3. $9 + 7 - 6 = 10$
4. $9 - 7 + 6 = 8$
5. $9 + 1 - 6 = 4$
6. $9 - 7 + 1 = 3$
7. $9 + 6 - 1 = 14$
8. $7 - 6 + 1 = 2$

13 How Big Is a Million?

1. 6,140,000 inches or 511,666.67 feet or 96.906566 miles (about 97 miles)
2. 2,739.726 years
3. 250 weeks

15 Multiplication Mix-Up

X	6	8	10	5	9	3	1	4	2	7
2	12	16	20	10	18	6	2	8	4	14
6	36	48	60	30	54	18	6	24	12	42
5	30	40	50	25	45	15	5	20	10	35
9	54	72	90	45	81	27	9	36	18	63
1	6	8	10	5	9	3	1	4	2	7
7	42	56	70	35	63	21	7	28	14	49
10	60	80	100	50	90	30	10	40	20	70
3	18	24	30	15	27	9	3	12	6	21
4	24	32	40	20	36	12	4	16	8	28
8	48	64	80	40	72	24	8	32	16	56

16 Visual Thinking

1. f and k
2. a. BIRD
   b. FISH
   c. WASH
   d. REAL
3. b and d

17 Sum Shapes

Answers may vary.

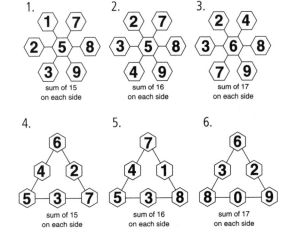

1. sum of 15 on each side
2. sum of 16 on each side
3. sum of 17 on each side
4. sum of 15 on each side
5. sum of 16 on each side
6. sum of 17 on each side

19 Who Am I?

1. 6
2. 17
3. 764
4. 45
5. 482

22 How Many Blocks?

1. 8
2. 9
3. 13
4. 24
5. 46
6. 46

23 Sum Strings of 16

15 solutions:

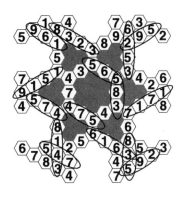

25 Largest–Smallest

1. Smallest: 1357; largest: 9875
2. Smallest: 2344; largest: 8744
3. Smallest: 22,357; largest: 87,753
4. Smallest: 35,667; largest: 87,766
5. Smallest: 23,355; largest: 99,755
6. Smallest: 345,667; largest: 977,665
7. Smallest: 123,344; largest: 876,544
8. Smallest: 233,455; largest: 877,655

26 Sum Shapes

Answers may vary.

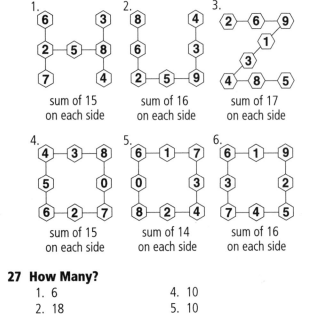

1. sum of 15 on each side
2. sum of 16 on each side
3. sum of 17 on each side
4. sum of 15 on each side
5. sum of 14 on each side
6. sum of 16 on each side

27 How Many?

1. 6
2. 18
3. 12
4. 10
5. 10
6. 9

29 Number Names
1. One hundred twenty-three
2. Four hundred fifty-six
4. Five hundred
5. Two hundred three
6. Eighty-seven
7. Four hundred forty-four
8. Two thousand twenty-one
9. Thirty-two thousand four hundred four
10. One million twenty thousand ninety-nine

30 Same Shapes
1. g and j
2. c and l
3. d and l
4. g and j
5. e and l
6. d and i
7. c and f
8. e and l

31 Juggling Digits
1. 11, 12, 13, 21, 22, 23, 31, 32, 33
2. 222, 224, 226, 242, 246, 262, 264, 422, 426, 462, 622, 624, 642
3. 1357, 1375, 1537, 1573, 1735, 1753, 3157, 3175, 3517, 3571, 3715, 3751, 5137, 5173, 5317, 5371, 5713, 5731, 7135, 7153, 7315, 7351, 7513, 7531

32 Which Circle Appears Larger?
Though the upper center circle may appear larger, they are actually exactly the same size.

33 Target Practice
Answers may vary but include:
1. 8 − 5 − 3 = 0
2. 9 + 8 − 5 = 12
3. 8 + 5 − 3 = 10
4. 9 + 8 − 3 = 14
5. 9 − 8 + 5 = 6
6. 9 + 3 − 8 = 4
7. 8 + 3 − 9 = 2
8. 9 − 5 + 3 = 7

35 Problems to Solve
1. 456, 457, 465, 467, 475, 476, 546, 547, 564, 567, 574, 576, 645, 647, 654, 657, 674, 675, 745, 746, 754, 756, 764, 765
2. The ball will bounce 0.25 meters high, or 25 centimeters.
3. Chuck is the youngest, Ann the oldest.

37 Puzzle Pieces
1. b and f
2. e and f
3. a and f

39 You Grade It
Answers provided here are the corrections students should make.
1. 228
2. C (correct)
3. 1148
4. C (correct)
5. C (correct)
6. 438.35
7. C (correct)
8. 1,200,000
9. 63,137,824,005

41 Crossnumber Puzzle

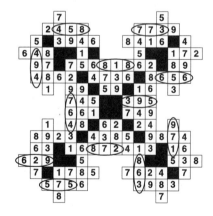

42 Even and Odd Number Patterns

Even-Odd Addition

+	0	1	2	3	4	5	6	7	8	9
0	E	O	E	O	E	O	E	O	E	O
1	O	E	O	E	O	E	O	E	O	E
2	E	O	E	O	E	O	E	O	E	O
3	O	E	O	E	O	E	O	E	O	E
4	E	O	E	O	E	O	E	O	E	O
5	O	E	O	E	O	E	O	E	O	E
6	E	O	E	O	E	O	E	O	E	O
7	O	E	O	E	O	E	O	E	O	E
8	E	O	E	O	E	O	E	O	E	O
9	O	E	O	E	O	E	O	E	O	E

Even-Odd Multiplication

X	0	1	2	3	4	5	6	7	8	9
0	E	E	E	E	E	E	E	E	E	E
1	E	O	E	O	E	O	E	O	E	O
2	E	E	E	E	E	E	E	E	E	E
3	E	O	E	O	E	O	E	O	E	O
4	E	E	E	E	E	E	E	E	E	E
5	E	O	E	O	E	O	E	O	E	O
6	E	E	E	E	E	E	E	E	E	E
7	E	O	E	O	E	O	E	O	E	O
8	E	E	E	E	E	E	E	E	E	E
9	E	O	E	O	E	O	E	O	E	O

Addition Conclusions

+	O	E
O	E	O
E	O	E

Multiplication Conclusions

X	O	E
O	O	E
E	E	E

43 Sum Strings
12 solutions, as indicated:

45 Same Shapes
Triangles: 8 and 22, 10 and 29
Squares: 17 and 24
Parallelograms: 7 and 27
Rectangles (that aren't squares): 9 and 30

46 Sum Shortcuts

Shortcuts will vary
1. 119 (7 × 17)
2. 169 (7 × 24 + 1)
3. 90 (3 × 30)
4. 140 labels (4 × 35)
5. 92 stamps (10 × 10 − 8)
6. 37 squares (9 × 4 + 1)
7. $13.30 (10 x 4 × $ 0.35 − $ 0.70)

47 Problems to Solve

1. Place one bar on either side of the balance scale. Designate these two bars as A and B. Repeat, using the other two bars, designated C and D. One of these pairings will yield an unbalanced scale. Then weigh one brick from the unbalanced pair against one brick from the balanced pair. If the result is balanced, then the counterfeit brick is the remaining brick from the unbalanced pair. For instance, if AB is unbalanced, while CD is balanced, try AC. If AC is balanced, then B is the counterfeit brick. If AC is unbalanced, then A is counterfeit.
2. 11 wins and 3 losses
3. 36 rectangles

48 Hexagon Puzzle

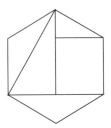

49 Target Practice

Answers may vary but may include:
1. 6 × 2 + 3 = 15
2. 3 × 2 + 6 = 12
3. 6 × 3 + 2 = 20
4. 6 × 2 − 3 = 9
5. 6 × 3 − 2 = 16
6. 3 × 2 − 6 = 0
7. 7 × 3 + 4 = 25
8. 4 × 7 − 3 = 25

51 Who Am I?

1. 5 (or −3)
2. 87
3. 11
4. 495
5. 198

53 How Many?

1. 8
2. 13
3. 45
4. 7
5. 14
6. 19

54 Tall Tales

1. Shortest
2. Tallest
3. Shortest
4. Jeff

(From tallest to shortest: Jeff, Les, Dave, Ken)

55 Being Observant

Answers will vary but may include:
1. Multiples of 7
2. Sum of the digits is 10.
3. Digits differ by 2
4. All contain at least one right angle.
5. Odd numbers
6. Cubes

57 Problems to Solve

1. Nancy to Kay: mother
   Kay to Barb: niece
   Barb to Annette: aunt
   Kate to Annette: cousin
2. The most popular number was 8.

58 How Many?

1. 5 squares, 11 rectangles
2. 12 rectangles
3. 3 rectangles, 12 triangles
4. 2 regular pentagons, 35 triangles
5. 4 squares, 12 triangles
6. 3 rectangles, 32 triangles

59 Grouping Numbers

1. (3 + 3) × 2 = 12
2. 3 + (3 × 2) = 9
3. 8 ÷ (2 − 1) = 8
4. (8 ÷ 2) − 1 = 3
5. (15 − 7) − 2 = 6
6. 15 − (7 − 2) = 10
7. (3 × 5) − 2 = 13
8. 3 × (5 − 2) = 9
9. (2 × 6) + 5 = 17
10. 2 × (6 + 5) = 22
11. (4 ÷ 2) × 2 = 4
12. 4 ÷ (2 × 2) = 1

61 Race Results

1. Margo won. Jane was second.
2. Number 3 won. Number 4 was second.
3. Red won the race.

62 Matchstick Puzzles

1.

2.

3.

63 Visual Fractions

1. Black, $\frac{3}{8}$; white, $\frac{5}{8}$
2. Black, $\frac{4}{9}$; white, $\frac{5}{9}$
3. Black, $\frac{2}{5}$; white, $\frac{3}{5}$
4. Black, $\frac{1}{4}$; white, $\frac{3}{4}$
5. Black, $\frac{2}{3}$; white, $\frac{1}{3}$
6. Black, $\frac{3}{5}$; white, $\frac{2}{5}$
7. Black, $\frac{3}{4}$; white, $\frac{1}{4}$
8. Black, $\frac{5}{8}$; white, $\frac{3}{8}$

On problems 9 through 16, the exact position of shaded shapes may vary. Here are some solutions:

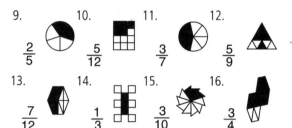

9. $\frac{2}{5}$ 10. $\frac{5}{12}$ 11. $\frac{3}{7}$ 12. $\frac{5}{9}$

13. $\frac{7}{12}$ 14. $\frac{1}{3}$ 15. $\frac{3}{10}$ 16. $\frac{3}{4}$

65 What Fractional Part?

1. $\frac{1}{2}$
2. $\frac{1}{3}$
3. $\frac{1}{2}$
4. $\frac{5}{9}$
5. $\frac{5}{9}$
6. $\frac{1}{2}$
7. $\frac{1}{9}$
8. $\frac{1}{9}$
9. $\frac{13}{18}$
10. $\frac{1}{3}$
11. $\frac{1}{3}$

66 Vertical Symmetry

1. In the first alphabet: A, H, I, M, O, T, U, V, W, X, Y.
   In the second alphabet: H, I, O, T.
2. Answers will vary but may include: HIM, TOY, MYTH, TOT, MAIM, MOAT.

67 Horizontal Symmetry

1. C, D, E, H, I, K, O, X (E, H, K, and X are not actually horizontally symmetrical in this particular font.)
2. Answers will vary but include: HEED, COOK, DECIDE, COKE.

70 Wheel of Fraction

THAT'S COOL

71 Polyominoes

These are the five different tetrominoes. The orientation of the answers may differ from these, but the relative arrangement of the squares should be the same.

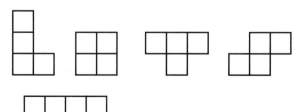

75 Target Practice

1. $(8 - 6) \times 7 = 14$
2. $9 \times (6 + 4) = 90$
3. $5 + (2 \times 6) = 17$
4. $4 \times (9 - 6) = 12$
5. $(5 + 6) \times 2 = 22$
6. $(9 - 8) \times 3 = 3$
7. $9 - (6 \div 2) = 6$
8. $8 \times (3 + 1) = 32$

77 Relationships

1. Less than
2. Heavier than
3. Identical to
4. On the right of
5. Aunt or uncle
6. One-third of
7. 5 less than
8. $A - C = B$
9. $C \div B = A$ or $C \div A = B$

79 Logic Loops

Answers may vary. Here are some examples:

1.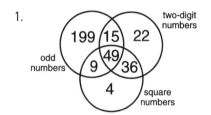

2.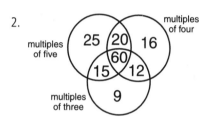

3.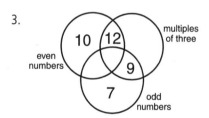

81 What Direction?

1. SE
2. NW
3. E
4. W
5. SE
6. N
7. NE
8. NW

85 One Tough Puzzle

Note to teacher: To facilitate discussion of solutions, number the vertices (1, 2, 3, 4, etc.) across, down, and so forth. This allows clearer references to specific portions of the figure.

1. 20 rectangles
2. 72 triangles
3. 17 squares
4. 57 parallelograms

More Smart Books

Locate the puzzle, activity, or challenge that interests you. Then match the corresponding numbers in the Smart Books to Check column with the numbered books on the facing page.

Page	Puzzles, Challenges, and Activities	Smart Books to Check (see page 103)
1	Tic-Tac-Number	5
2	Visual: Black or White Arrows?	1, 37
4	Which One Differs?	34
6	The T Puzzle	34
8	Number Patterns	30
10	Visual: Three Kaleidoscopes	10, 13
11	Target Practice	26, 33
12	Drawing Patterns	24, 34
13	How Big Is a Million?	30
14	Visual: Rotating Triangles	27
16	Visual Thinking	24, 34
17	Sum Shapes	31
18	Geometric Patterns in Quilts	6
19	Who Am I?	26, 36
20	Visual: Making Paper Snowflakes	7, 15
21	Making Paper Snowflakes	7, 15
22	How Many Blocks?	12
23	Sum Strings of 16	26, 33
24	Visual: Rotating Ellipses	24, 34
26	Sum Shapes	26, 33
27	How Many?	24, 34
30	Same Shapes	24, 34
31	Juggling Digits	30

Page	Puzzles, Challenges, and Activities	Smart Books to Check (see page 103)
32	Visual: Which Circle Appears Larger?	1, 37
33	Target Practice	26, 33
34	Scale Drawing	21
35	Problems to Solve	22, 30
36	Visual: Geometric Patterns	28
37	Puzzle Pieces	24, 34
38	Straight-Line Curves	27, 29
40	Visual: Checkered Hexagons	27
42	Even and Odd Number Patterns	22, 30
43	Sum Strings	31
44	Photos: Geometry in Nature	17
45	Same Shapes	24, 34
47	Problems to Solve	22, 30
48	Hexagon Puzzle	34
49	Target Practice	26, 33
50	Drawing Patterns	24, 34
51	Who Am I?	26, 36
53	How Many?	24, 34
54	Tall Tales	36
55	Being Observant	22, 30
56	Visual: Rotate This Page	1, 37
57	Problems to Solve	22, 30
58	How Many?	24, 34
59	Grouping Numbers	26, 33

Page	Puzzles, Challenges, and Activities	Smart Books to Check (see page 103)
60	Visual: Geometric Patterns	28
61	Race Results	36
62	Matchstick Puzzles	4
64	Logos	2
66	Vertical Symmetry	2
67	Horizontal Symmetry	2
69	A Good Turn	2, 13
71	Polyominoes	8, 19
72	Visual: Star Designs	23, 25
73	Creating a Design	23, 25
74	Visual: Shrinking Stars	27
75	Target Practice	28, 33
76	Visual: Shrinking Triangles	27
77	Relationships	36
78	Visual: Line Designs	27, 29
79	Logic Loops	36
80	Visual: Geometric Patterns	28
82	Photos: Arcs and Arches	17
83	Try Tiling	28
84	Visual: Six Tribars	1, 9
85	One Tough Puzzle	24, 34
86	Visual: Rose of Black and White Circles	27

1. Block, J. R., and H. E. Yuker. *Can You Believe Your Eyes?* New York: Gardner Press, 1989.

2. Britton, Jill. *Symmetry and Tessellations.* Parsippany, NJ: Dale Seymour Publications, 2000.

3. Brooke, Maxey. *150 Puzzles in Crypt-Arithmetic.* New York: Dover Publications, 1969.

4. Brooke, Maxey. *Tricks, Games, and Puzzles with Matches.* New York: Dover Publications, 1973.

5. Clark, Dave. *More Tic-Tac-Toe Math.* Parsippany, NJ: Dale Seymour Publications, 1996.

6. Cohen, Luanne Seymour. *Quilt Design Masters.* Parsippany, NJ: Dale Seymour Publications, 1996.

7. Davidson, Patricia, and Robert Willcut. *Spatial Problem Solving.* Parsippany, NJ: Cuisenaire Co. of America, 1984.

8. Duby, Marjorie. *Try It! Pentaminoes.* Parsippany, NJ: Cuisenaire Co. of America, 1992.

9. Ernst, Bruno. *Adventures with Impossible Figures.* New York: Parkwest Publications, 1987.

10. Finkel, Norma Yvette, and Leslie Finkel. *Kaleidoscope Designs and How to Create Them.* New York: Dover Publications, 1980.

11. Kenneway, Eric. *Complete Origami.* New York: St. Martin's Press, 1987.

12. Kremer, Ron. *Exploring with Squares and Cubes.* Parsippany, NJ: Dale Seymour Publications, 1989.

13. Kroner, Louis R. *Slides, Flips, and Turns.* Parsippany, NJ: Dale Seymour Publications, 1984.

14. McKim, Robert. *Thinking Visually.* Parsippany, NJ: Dale Seymour Publications, 1997.

15. Murray, William, and Francis Rigney. *Paper Folding for Beginners.* New York: Dover Publications, 1960.

16. Neale, Robert, and Thomas Hull. *Origami, Plain and Simple.* New York: St. Martin's Press, 1994.

17. Norwich, John Julius, ed., et al. *Great Architecture of the World.* New York: Da Capo Press, 1991.

18. Pearce, Peter, and Susan Pearce. *Polyhedra Primer.* Parsippany, NJ: Dale Seymour Publications, 1978.

19. Picciotto, Henri. *Pentamino Activities, Lessons, and Puzzles.* Chicago: Creative Publications, 1986.

20. Pollard, Jeanne. *Building Toothpick Bridges.* Parsippany, NJ: Dale Seymour Publications, 1985.

21. Rozell, Paula. *Plotting Pictures: Grades 5–8.* Parsippany, NJ: Dale Seymour Publications, 1997.

22. Seymour, Dale, Mary Laycock, Ruth Heller, and Bob Larsen. *Aftermath* (series). Chicago: Creative Publications, 1970.

23. Seymour, Dale, and Schadler Reuben. *Creative Constructions.* Rev. ed. Chicago: Creative Publications, 1974.

24. Seymour, Dale, and Ed Beardslee. *Critical Thinking Activities* (series). Parsippany, NJ: Dale Seymour Publications, 1988.

25. Seymour, Dale. *Geometric Design.* Parsippany, NJ: Dale Seymour Publications, 1988.

26. Seymour, Dale, and John Gregory. *I'm a Number Game.* Chicago: Creative Publications, 1978.

27. Seymour, Dale. *Introduction to Line Designs.* Parsippany, NJ: Dale Seymour Publications, 1992.

28. Seymour, Dale, and Jill Britton. *Introduction to Tessellations.* Parsippany, NJ: Dale Seymour Publications, 1989.

29. Seymour, Dale, Linda Silvey, and Joyce Snider. *Line Designs.* Rev. ed. Chicago: Creative Publications, 1974.

30. Seymour, Dale. *Problem Parade.* Parsippany, NJ: Dale Seymour Publications, 1984.

31. Seymour, Dale. *Sum Puzzles.* Chicago: Creative Publications, 1979.

32. Seymour, Dale. *Tangramath.* Chicago: Creative Publications, 1971.

33. Seymour, Dale, and Margo Seymour. *Target Practice* (series). Parsippany, NJ: Dale Seymour Publications, 1993.

34. Seymour, Dale. *Visual Thinking Cards* (series). Parsippany, NJ: Dale Seymour Publications, 1983.

35. Sherard, Wade H., III. *Cooperative Informal Geometry.* Parsippany, NJ: Dale Seymour Publications, 1995.

36. Sherard, Wade H., III. *Logic Number Problems.* Parsippany, NJ: Dale Seymour Publications, 1997.

37. Simon, Seymour. *The Optical Illusions Book.* New York: Beech Tree Books, 1976.

Smart Math Web Sites

In the time it takes to publish this book, a list of Web sites could easily become a bit out of date. With that caveat, here are sites that offer more mathematical puzzles, challenges, and beautiful images. If you find a site no longer available, try links from another site to newer sites on related topics. Explore!

Bullpup Math Resources. A middle-school site with toothpick (matchstick) puzzles, problem-of-the-day offerings, links to online math-problem contests, and links to online puzzle "rings" (strings of Web sites).
http://www.highland.madison.k12.il.us/jbasden/

Enchanted Mind. Visual and logic puzzles, such as tangrams, pentaminoes, pyramids; variety from National Center for Creativity. Online and printable puzzles.
http://enchantedmind.com/puzzle.htm

Fibonacci and the Golden Section. Explanations, a page of easier Fibonacci puzzles, and applications in art, architecture, and music.
http://www.ee.surrey.ac.uk/Personal/R.Knott/ Fibonacci/fib.html

Geometry Through Art.
http://forum.swarthmore.edu/~sarah/shapiro/

Interactive Mathematics Miscellany and Puzzles. Online and printable puzzles and games, fun even for those who "hate" math; also available on CD-ROM.
http://www.cut-the-knot.com/

Magic Squares. Unit for upper elementary and middle-school students.
http://forum.swarthmore.edu/alejandre/magic. square.html

Math Forum (Swarthmore College). Showcases great activities on specific math concepts, such as dividing by zero, magic squares, polyhedra, Pascal's triangle, making tessellations, famous math problems. Links to many math problems and puzzles on the Internet.
http://forum.swarthmore.edu/.

Mathematical Problem Solving Task Centres. Monthly mathematically oriented problem for various grade levels, with past problems cataloged. From Mathematical Association of Victoria, Australia.
http://www.srl.rmit.edu.au/mav/PSTC/general/ index.html

Pascal's Triangle. Lessons and worksheets.
http://forum.swarthmore.edu/workshops/usi/ pascal/pascal_lessons.html#lessons

Perspective Drawing, Moebius Strip, Polyhedra, and Spreadsheets.
http://forum.swarthmore.edu/sum95/math_and/

Symbolic Sculpture and Mathematics. Gallery of mathematical sculptures by John Robinson (such as on page 68). Math explanations and construction tips on structures such as rings, bands, knots, and fractals.
http://www.bangor.ac.uk/SculMath/

Symmetry and Pattern: The Art of Oriental Carpets.
http://forum.swarthmore.edu/geometry/rugs/

Tessellation Tutorials. Tutorials teach students how to tessellate (somewhat in the style of M. C. Escher) using common software, templates, or simple straightedge and compass.
http://forum.swarthmore.edu/sum95/suzanne/ tess.intro.html

University of Minnesota Geometry Center Graphics Archive. Includes fractals, digital art, 3-D art, advanced topics such as tilings.
http://www.geom.umn.edu/graphics/

Virtual Polyhedra. Collection of over 1000 virtual-reality polyhedra to explore, with classroom ideas for making and exploring polyhedra.
http://www.li.net/~george/virtual-polyhedra/ vp.html

World of Escher. Examples of Escher's work, background, and an annual tessellation contest for students, with winning images.
http://www.worldofescher.com/